CONTENTS

W9-CNX-911

1. CHILDHOOD

Our main home was in Leningrad, the second largest city in Russia. One particular summer, however, my parents rented a small wooden dacha in Wyritza, a small town about sixty kilometers away. They decided the house must be on the banks of the river Oredesch. "It might be a little inconvenient," said Mama, "but we'll have a wonderful view!"

When I started school, the doctor had said to Mama, "Your little girl is not strong. It would be good if she could live away from the city for a year. You will easily find another school for her in the country. It wouldn't do you any harm to stay away from the city, either, Madam," he continued sternly. "You are looking pale."

Everyone in our family loved Wyritza, so in the

circumstances it was natural that my parents moved there. It took the old steam locomotive two hours to make the journey, and I was thrilled. The following winter I would be able to ski and skate directly from the front steps of the house.

A German lady lived opposite us. Her small wooden house stood very near the river. Mama said that you could tell she was German because she spoke Russian with a German accent. She was already very old, but she always looked neat and very cheerful.

Once, when we met on my way to the river, she said, "Wouldn't you like to learn German, little one? Everything we learn in this life may come in useful."

Of course I said yes. I found it very exciting to be in contact with a German. She had been born in Germany, in a town on the river Elbe, but, she explained, Russia was her new home.

"In Germany," she told me, "there is another large and beautiful river like the Oredesch, called the Rhine. The wonderful German poet Heinrich Heine wrote poems about it. One of the poems tells how a girl called Lorelei sits on a rock above the Rhine, combing her golden hair. But now," she said sadly, "Heine's poems are burned on rubbish heaps in Germany."

I found this very strange and asked why people were doing this. The German lady answered sternly, "You'll understand when you are older," and started to teach me the old saying, "Never put off till tomorrow, what can be done today."

She knew many such folk sayings. Soon we greeted each other only in German: "Guten Morgen," "Guten Tag," "Guten Abend." And she always reminded me, "Everything we learn in this life may come in useful."

April 1941. I am about to end my fifth year at school with "excellent." I am very happy. Yesterday I even bought a little notebook and called it "A Diary of Happy Days." In this diary I have written everything I can remember about myself and my family since I was five, and I have decided to record every good thing that ever happens to me.

June 22, 1941. Papa has come from town unexpectedly. We weren't expecting him yet because he was supposed to stay in hospital for another fortnight. He has a stomach ulcer. Now they have told him to "stay in bed at home." Papa is depressed, but not because of the stomach ulcer. He has had that for ages. He says, "Germany has declared war on us."

I debated for a long time whether I should write about this day or not — after all, my diary is only for happy days. But then I did write about it because the summer holidays *are* a happy time.

This evening the boys said we should play Soldiers and Battles. We ran around like mad things, even though we are all thirteen years old.

July 10, 1941. Today Mama told us that food is becoming more difficult to find. She said that there are mushrooms in the woods already, and we should go to gather some. Papa is in bed. Mama had to call the doctor again last night.

The woods are not far from our house. We took my little sister Olja with us. She is two, and very active for her age.

It was lovely in the woods. We gathered two baskets of mushrooms and ate our fill of berries. We came out of the woods at the Siwersker highway, and from there it's only a short walk home. But Olja was tired and kicked her legs in the air.

Mama took the two baskets of mushrooms and said she would go on ahead to wash them. Olja and I were to follow her more slowly. It wasn't long before she was out of sight.

Olja began to whimper "carry me," so I picked her up. She is very heavy. Mama says that all the babies were big in the year Olja was born, but she was the biggest and prettiest baby of the lot — all the nurses in the maternity ward said so.

With a big effort I gave my sister a piggy-back.

Then I saw troop carriers and military vehicles coming toward us down the highway. They were bearing down on us incredibly fast.

I had never seen so many soldiers in Wyritza, or anywhere else for that matter. I stood still and watched the speeding vehicles with their Red Army soldiers, and the trucks carrying rocket launchers and machine-guns.

The soldiers were covered in dust and looked very tired. When they stopped, they looked sadly at Olja and me.

I felt very uneasy. Then suddenly everything fell apart in front of my eyes. Someone yelled an order, "Take cover!," and before I could gather my wits I heard a terrible droning above me, and a piercing wail. In seconds the road was empty.

Where have the soldiers gone? I wondered. I leant my head back and looked up into the sky. Where was that dreadful sound coming from?

Something black appeared directly above my head. It shut out the sun. An airplane marked with swastikas screamed above me, and two helmeted heads peered out. They looked terrifying. Then came shots, a burst of gunfire, machine-gun salvos.

I ran headlong through the smoke, beside myself with fear, crying, "Mama, Mama!"

An eerie silence followed after the noise, as if

nothing had happened. I stopped under a tree very near our house and held Olja tight. Mama was running up and down the terrace by the steps, shouting, "Tanja, little Tanja, where are you?"

People were scurrying about, screaming. The soldiers reappeared from the ground as if by magic and ran to their cars and trucks which then roared off. Many houses had had their roofs damaged, but our house came through unscathed.

So today I have recorded a very unhappy day in my diary. The war has reached Wyritza.

Later a neighbor came to see us and said that our soldiers are surrounded and trying to break out. That's why the troops are moving so fast.

Mama is upset. She hopes so much that our soldiers won't be taken prisoner. But Papa says we shouldn't start to panic: Maybe our troops are just changing positions.

August 1, 1941. Now we are being bombed every night. I wake up screaming each time and tumble head over heels into the cellar. Mama follows calmly, hugging Olja to her in silence. Olja cries. Whenever a bomb explodes, I scream out, "I want to live! I want to live!"

Mama whispers, "Soon, little Tanja, soon it'll be over. Be brave."

My father won't go into the cellar. It's a matter of principle, he says. But what principle does he mean? I think he simply finds it too hard. He can hardly walk any more. He is ill, and it is not just a stomach ulcer now.

August 15, 1941. Our dacha has been burnt down in the bombing. We managed to get out unhurt, however, and were even able to rescue a few bits and pieces from the wreckage.

Now we have moved into the Platonows' house. We would have been moving in there soon, anyway. The Platonows are Walja's parents. Walja is a boy I became good friends with this summer. He is fifteen years old and seems very grown up.

Back in July, Sofja Iwanowna, Walja's mother, had come to see us. She said, "Falja, we are leaving the dacha soon. Why don't you move in? It is large and warm, and it has a garden, and even a goat. Goats' milk is good for children."

At the time Mama tried to persuade Sofja Iwanowna to wait and not to spoil the holidays for the children. Perhaps everything would sort itself out anyway, and if not, then we could all leave together in the autumn.

It was obvious that Sofja Iwanowna was very reluctant to leave the dacha, but she shook her head sadly and sighed, "No no. My husband thinks we must go. We can't risk staying here. He is a member of the Communist party and needed in Leningrad. If everything does work out all right, we'll be back here by the autumn."

We didn't move into the Platonows' house as soon as they left in July. Mama didn't want to. So Sofja Iwanowna brought us the goat and left the keys with us "just in case."

Now the keys have come in very handy. The Platonows' house is not far, so it hasn't been difficult to move our belongings. We have simply taken whatever was left over from the fire with us.

The Platonows' house stands right on the Siwersker highway, and now I can see everything that is going on there. Our troops drive by. Father still doesn't believe that our men are in retreat and growls, "How can anyone think that our soldiers are retreating! They are regrouping for the counter-strike."

Perhaps he says this because he is afraid that he won't be able to flee if he has to.

"Tell me, are you really retreating?" Mama asks the soldiers on the highway. "Are the Germans nearby? What shall we do? Give us some advice."

"Get out, get out!" says one.

"Go to the North, quickly!" agree the others.

Mama is frustrated. It is the middle of August; soon it will be autumn. And Father has had another attack. How can we flee? How?

September 7, 1941. Things are looking bad. A few days ago people carrying bags, rucksacks, and children began to come along the highway. The trains to Wyritza stopped.

Mother packed a large bundle of warm clothes and we dressed ourselves and set off, hoping to flee the advancing German troops. Father took a walking stick and hobbled after us.

We walked in the direction of Antropschino. From here, so they said, trains were still going to Leningrad. But how would we get through to Antropschino? "It is about thirty kilometers," said Mama.

The other people hurried, but we could only go slowly. Father held us up, and also Olja, and I wasn't exactly fast. Mama carried the heavy bundle on her back.

By evening we had walked fifteen kilometers, but then we came into heavy crossfire. We meant to take a shortcut, but got lost and found ourselves back on the Siwersker highway by morning, only a couple of kilometers from our house.

We arrived back home totally exhausted. Mama

threw the bundle from her shoulders and said, "I'm not going anywhere. I won't move from this place. Wild horses won't drag me away!"

For two days Wyritza stayed as silent as the grave. On the third day we were startled by a constant, rhythmic throbbing. We looked out of the windows: A long line of black Panzer tanks marked with · swastikas were driving up the highway.

"The fascists!" whispered Mama fearfully. I still couldn't believe it. Perhaps they were our tanks?

But they were not. They were alien. The tanks were new and spotless. A soldier stood at attention on each one, clean-shaven and smart. They stood there so proudly, so superior, as if they were saying, "Here we are, your conquerors. From now on you will belong to us forever."

Two people ran toward the tanks and gave the conquerors flowers. One of the soldiers accepted them and gave a greeting.

"But that was ———." Mama shook her head. "I would never have thought he would give flowers to the enemy."

September 15, 1941. This morning I was woken up by the sound of groaning. I went out onto the road. There I saw rows of prisoners of war, nearly all wounded. Some were bandaged, others bound up with rags. The blood seeped out red. . . .

Those who were very weak marched in the middle; those who were stronger stayed in the outside rows. The ones on the outside kept the whole line on its feet. Again and again the columns broke down; the wounded couldn't stay upright. But the guards yelled, "Silence! Quick, march!" and beat the men on the outside with their rifle butts.

The sound of groaning hovered over the whole troop. The groans startled the horses drawing the carts full of dying men. Where were they being taken?

Sobbing, I ran into the house, to Mama, but she had also been staring out of the window all this time. She dried my tears with her apron and said, "So much blood, so much blood, Tanja! Those poor boys, their unhappy mothers . . ."

I am writing down what I have learned today. War is not just a word. War is terrible and full of blood.

Father, lying on his bed, talks to himself. "Don't you worry, Russia will fight back. We're occupied, it's true, but Russia will still fight. Russia will not give in."

Papa is right — we are occupied. We are only allowed out until dusk. Mushroom and berry gathering is forbidden. But there is nothing else to eat. Patrols come regularly and force their way into our house. They strip the beds and turn the sheets inside out. "Partisans? Partisans?" they shout, and aim their rifles at Papa.

I somehow explain, "He's ill. He's ill."

It's a good thing that I learned German; it is coming in useful.

October 30, 1941. When autumn came, we slaughtered the goat and ate meat for a whole week. Everything from the garden was eaten up ages ago. Now Mama collects all the bits and pieces in the house and walks as far as she can in daylight to Dowschowo village, twelve kilometers from Wyritza. She barters everything we have for potatoes. Soon there will come a day when we have nothing left to barter.

Tragedies are happening outside our windows. Today the prisoners of war, who don't get even the smallest amount of food from the Germans for their exhausting labor, caught a dog on the street. That is amazing in itself: Dogs disappeared from here long ago.

They ate this one raw! Mama was upset.

"You shouldn't eat meat raw," she said. "You can die from it."

But Papa only murmured, "So what? It's all over. Everything's over," again and again.

December 1, 1941. We are starving. A few days ago Mama became so weak that she couldn't walk to find food any more. We lay on our beds, as Papa had done for so long, and prepared to die.

Perhaps dying isn't so terrible, I said to myself, as long as it happens quickly.

A white snowflake floated past the window, but everything was going dark. I whispered incoherently and sank down into blackness. The last thing I knew was that someone had fallen to the floor. "Mama?"

I didn't hear the answer.

In the distance I thought I could hear a voice, and it was coming closer. "Tanja, Tanja, open your mouth and swallow."

I swallowed. Something warm flowed into my body and I opened my eyes.

Mama was bending over me and spooning soup into my mouth. "Swallow, Tanja, swallow." I swallowed again. The soup tasted very good. Mama murmured again and again, "Eat, eat!"

"Where did you get it, Mama? What is it?"

"Don't ask, just eat, eat . . ."

Later I found out the sad story. Maschka is dead. Maschka, my beloved cat. Now I only have her photograph, which shows me holding her in my arms. Part of the photograph was singed when I rescued it from our burning house.

I had found the little wild cat the year before and had bound up her wounded paw. Maschka was grateful and always came to meet me at the corner on my way back from school.

Now she was gone. Mama had pushed death back for a while longer. But for how long?

"We'll think of something. One must fight to live," whispered Mama faintly.

Three days after we had eaten the last of the soup, Mama said, "Get up, Pjotr. I have brought a piece of birch wood. We will grate it small and make it into gruel."

Father got up with difficulty, and we started to grate the wood. Mama cooked a porridge with the strands and let it simmer for five hours. When we had eaten it, we thought we would die on the spot. For twenty-four hours our stomachs were in revolt. Father groaned terribly. Then it was over. We had survived.

January 6, 1942. Again we lay down and waited for the end. Then three men came into the house: German soldiers. They looked into all the rooms and then said, "This is where the offices will go."

The offices took up two empty rooms. At least they didn't kick us out of the house.

That same evening an elderly German came into

our room. He explained, using his hands and feet, that he made coats for the soldiers. Then he pulled a loaf of bread from under his jacket and gave it to Mama. "Bread . . . children . . ." he said, and put his finger on his lips. We understood. He meant that we shouldn't tell anyone about it.

The tailor came to our room every day from then on, as soon as everyone else had left the offices, and he always brought a loaf of bread. We grew stronger and got up from our beds — except for Papa, of course, and Olja. Olja's legs had become useless while she was starving, and she could not walk or stand. Now, like Papa, she had to lie down all the time.

The tailor looked at Olja and her blue eyes for a long time, stood up, and shook his head. Then he brought her some sugar.

We survived January quite well, but at the end of January the tailor was suddenly called up to the front. He came into our room one last time and brought bread and barley. He looked at us sadly for a while, and then he shook his head in despair.

"He is a good man," said Mama, when the tailor had left us. "Not so young any more and he still has to go to the front."

"He is even destroying his own people; even his own," Papa muttered quietly. He meant Hitler, of course.

The tailor had given us enough barley and bread for a whole week and had also left us various remnants of cloth left over from the German soldiers' coats. Mama immediately started to make me a vest out of them, because I was always cold and we had already swapped all our warm clothes for bread.

Then we ran out of food again.

February 12, 1942. We had had nothing to eat for many days. Not even the smallest crumb.

I heard Mama's voice from the corner of the room opposite. "What shall we do now, Pjotr?"

My sick father lay helplessly on the big bed. He could take no part in this struggle.

"Now what, Pjotr?" Mama repeated. "Everything we had in the house has been bartered. Soon people won't be interested in dealing any more. Rumor has it they don't have enough for themselves. Those who aren't working for the Germans are lying sick and bloated. More people are dying in their own homes every day. It's only those who fled to the corn-growing regions who have saved themselves from starvation."

"I don't know what to do, Falja," answered my father in a weak voice. "Think of some way to save yourselves and don't think of me. I am at the end of my strength now. My days are numbered."

My mother fought with her tears, Olja sitting on her lap.

"But Mama, why don't we go where the corn is, too?" I asked.

Mother just shook her head. "It's too late, Tanja; we wouldn't make it. You can see that for yourself. What would we do with Father? And Olja's legs are useless. We wouldn't survive the frost. We would freeze to death along the way."

"Then I will go on my own," I said decidedly. "Find something that I can swap for some corn. I'll go and get the corn and bring it back."

Now Mama broke down in tears. "What are you saying, Tanja? You, all on your own? You wouldn't survive it. The journey is dangerous, and you are so weak you couldn't even manage the distance. So many people have already set out and frozen to death along the way."

But I wouldn't give up. "Pack a bag for me," I said. "I'll set out tomorrow. We don't have time to wait any longer."

The next day I got up very early. Mother lit the fire in the stove and put the water on to boil. We had nothing whatever to eat.

A sled stood in the hall. Mama put the small sack with our last few remaining pieces of cloth on top of it. Tears streamed down her face. "I am so afraid that I will never see you again. Please stay here, Tanja."

But I had no intention of changing my mind. "I'll hurry, Mama, you'll see. I'll soon come back and bring lots of corn with me."

I drank the hot water and pulled the sled out onto the front steps. Dawn was breaking. A frosty February day was beginning. For one brief moment I was scared. How far would I get in this frost, with not even a piece of bread to eat? But to stay here would mean starvation. . . . No, never! Not that. I didn't want to die.

I went through the gate and walked swiftly along the Siwersker highway in the direction of the station. There was no one to be seen far and wide, not even a German patrol. When would I be coming back? Would I ever see Mama again? Enough! I knew I mustn't think about things like that. I must only think about bread, nothing else.

I reached the railway line and turned right, following the track. Mama had told me, "The first station is Sluditzy. It's eleven kilometers away. But don't stop there — in Sluditzy the people are also starving. Go further, to Nowinka. Nowinka is bigger. Apparently the townsfolk there gave all the refugees potatoes in the autumn. What it's like now, I don't know. But don't stop, Tatjana, until you are in Nowinka."

That's what I'd do, I decided. Eleven kilometers in one day would not be enough. I would have to cover at least twenty a day, otherwise those at home wouldn't survive long enough to see me come back with the corn. In any case, the corn regions only started after about one hundred kilometers. Before then, nobody would sell you food. They didn't have any themselves.

To my own amazement, I set off quite strongly. Huge fir trees towered above me on either side of the railway line. Powdered with snow and drooping with icicles, they really looked enchanted. Gazing at them was both disturbing and beautiful.

I don't know how long I walked, but all of a sudden I felt my legs giving way from tiredness. It was very cold, and getting colder. There were no people anywhere. Where was Sluditzy? If only I were there!

At last, just as my strength was beginning to fail me, the first houses came into view. Saved in the nick of time. Even though I felt dead tired, I was happy. But what now? How would I go on? I had only managed eleven kilometers and I was already exhausted. Should I turn back? No, I must rest in Sluditzy, and then we would see.

I knocked at the first house I came to, a large and

beautiful building with smoke curling from its chimneys. I was looking forward to drinking some hot water to warm me up a little. Perhaps I could even sleep. . . .

No chance of that. They didn't even open the door. I saw only a shadow flit across the curtains.

I knocked at the second house, and the third. But either they wouldn't open the door at all, or they told me that there was nowhere for me to stay; all the houses were full to overflowing. And that was probably the truth. At first the villagers had taken in the refugees and tried to help them as best they could. But then more and more came, many dirty and full of lice and bloated with hunger. And some of those to whom they gave shelter in the evening were found the next morning dead in their beds. But I only learned all this later on.

At the time, as I realized that I was gradually freezing to death so close to warmth and shelter, I became utterly frustrated. If I don't get some hot water to drink right now, I thought, I'll keel over and freeze in the middle of the village.

Then, just as I had given up hope, somebody did let me into his house. It was the poorest and meanest little hut in the whole village. An old man lived there. He said that he had only recently buried his wife. She had died of hunger, but he would survive for a while longer.

"But it's bitterly cold, my little house," he continued, as if he wanted to apologize. "At night the cold comes straight in, so the water in the buckets turns to ice. Come to the hearth, little one, and thaw yourself out. You are quite stiff with cold already. It seems you can't even move your tongue any more."

It was really true. My tongue was frozen stiff and my teeth chattered so much that I could only speak by making a big effort. I leant against the warm brick stove, and the old man continued, "I'll just heat up some water for you, but don't expect anything else; there's nothing left. I am starving, too."

Gradually I began to revive. I thought about my future. I would probably survive the next day, but then? How was I going to live through this cold without any food? And finding a place to stay was obviously almost impossible. But as I warmed up and drank the hot water, I pushed these dark thoughts aside. I was so exhausted I was ready to collapse.

The old man had other people staying with him too: a young woman and her child. The old man had told them to crawl on top of the huge brick stove to sleep.

"And you — what's your name? Tatjana? Right,

Tatjana, lie down on this bench. I don't even have a bed for you! Everything that we had saved before the war went long ago, swapped for a piece of bread while my wife was still alive. Now there is nothing left to swap.

"Where are you going, little one?" he continued. "You will die. The people in the villages are already cutting themselves off from refugees. They don't have anything left themselves, but you still keep coming."

The old man's voice shook with fury. "The devil take you, you cursed fascist!" he cried. "Did you have to invade Russia? Things had improved before the war; we had some quite reasonable farms. Before that, after the last World War, there was no peace at all: first enemy troops, then civil war, then bad harvests. And now that damned fascist comes visiting! Oh, Russia will never find peace."

The old man grumbled on as he got himself ready for bed, but soon he fell silent.

I stretched myself out on the bench. It was long but narrow, and I didn't know where to put my arms, which hung down on either side. In the end I crossed them over my chest, like they do with dead people. My only blanket was my coat. It was a very uncomfortable bed, but tiredness overwhelmed me and I quickly fell asleep.

I woke up while it was still dark. I couldn't move. Had I been frozen to the bench? I wondered, horrified. But then I realized that only my clothes had frozen, and my back was numb from lying on the hard bench.

I stood up with difficulty. My whole body hurt; my legs had gone to sleep and wouldn't obey me any more. How could I continue my journey like this?

A thought flashed through my head: Turn back! But where to? Starvation was waiting for me at home. I had to flee. I had to flee starvation as quickly as possible.

The child on top of the brick stove was crying. The old man threw chunks of ice into a copper kettle. Even the water in the buckets had frozen solid overnight.

While I rubbed my back and warmed myself with hot water, I made up my mind. If I was going to die, then it would be on my journey. There was no turning back.

The old man said, "Another thirty, forty kilometers, Tatjana, then you might be able to get something to eat. Until then, don't count on it. The next thirty kilometers are tough. There are people dying every day. And finding shelter overnight will be hard. Here is a crust for your journey. It's only flattened grass, but even so, at least you'll have something to chew on. I would love to give you more, but there is really nothing left, not even the tiniest morsel."

I thanked him for everything, and left the hut. I didn't walk — no, I flew forward. I would probably still last for one more day. One more day of hunger, and then, according to the old man, rescue. If only I could travel more quickly. If only those dangerous kilometers were behind me.

After about two hours I came to the village of Nowinka, in which I had intended to spend the previous night. It was strange: On the second day of my journey I was striding out much more strongly and quickly, as if I had found my rhythm.

But after I had walked for fifteen kilometers, I began to feel dreadfully tired again, even though it was still light.

All this time I had been walking through a forest. The path was narrow and well used. Many people had obviously already taken it to the corn regions, but now there wasn't a soul to be seen.

The path wandered through the trees, between high, thickly planted firs whose branches met above it. It was dark, and suddenly I was afraid. What if a wolf appeared around the next corner? Where would I go? Up a tree? People said that many wolves still prowled here, carrying on their grisly business in the dense forest. And I was alone, completely alone.

I was afraid to stop, but hunger had been gnawing at me mercilessly for some time. Somehow I must make myself stronger. I fought back my fear, sat on the sled, and unpacked the crust which the old man had given me. It was frozen solid.

I had just bitten off a corner when I saw a man lying directly ahead of me. He was curled up against the cold, his glassy eyes staring at me.

The next minute it hit me: He was dead.

Horror gripped me. A man had fallen over here and never got up again. That could happen to me. I must leave this brooding forest quickly, quickly!

I stuffed the rest of the crust into my mouth, jumped up — desperately trying not to look — and ran away as quickly as I could. I no longer felt hungry and tired. Panic drove me onward. Where was the village, where was it? Why didn't it come? If only this terrible forest would come to an end.

At last, around a corner, I glimpsed a large village. It was only now that I realized just how tired I was. I was bathed in sweat and my legs were giving way. I had the feeling that I couldn't even manage the few steps separating me from the houses at the edge of the village.

But somehow I did manage it, and I was allowed to stay the night at the first house I knocked at. Only then did I realize that I had traveled thirty kilometers. How on earth had I done it?

This time the family who gave me shelter were cobblers. The master of the house was still a young man, but he had lost his legs. In the main room, beds had been pushed against the walls. The room smelt of newly cured leather. The cobbler obviously made shoes here, too.

The family gave me hot herb tea to drink and a few piping hot potatoes to eat. It was a real feast. I hadn't eaten so well for many months, ever since Wyritza was occupied.

After supper, the cobbler set to work. While he hammered a new heel onto a boot he said, "As you can see, little sister, I was wounded on the third day of the war and sent home. Little did I know that the Germans were closing in here, too. Still, we're not beaten yet. Though, to be honest, the whole thing is a mess. The war, this awful war, has changed all our lives, and no one knows when it will end. It's going to be a while till it's over, as far as I can see. But there's one good thing, at least there are fewer Germans here now. They probably need all the help they can get for the fight at Leningrad. That means the Germans can't be doing so well.

"Here," he continued. "Take a few leather soles. You might be able to swap them for something on your journey. I can't give you anything more. I feel sorry for you, little sister. You may well die, but you're very brave — and angry, I know."

They bedded me down on the floor and gave me a thick fur coverlet so that I was able to get warm in the night. As I fell asleep I thought, what friendly people I've met! I hope I meet many more good people on my travels.

When I woke up, I was convinced that I could make it to the cornfields. My hosts, who had warmed me up and given me new hope, even gave me some food for my journey.

The cobbler also gave me some advice. "Go quickly, Tanja. The next forty kilometers will be hard, but then the corn regions begin. Mind you, they say the people there already have everything that can be bartered, from carpets to mirrors. However, perhaps you'll be lucky and find some good folk."

That day I again walked many kilometers. Occasionally people gave me a piece of bread or a potato along the way. That gave me strength, and I strode out more energetically.

One village followed another, little ones and big ones. Tschastscha was far behind me; now I was passing Tscholowo. Should I stop here and sleep? Smoke drifted welcomingly from the chimneys. It was lovely and warm in the farmhouses, and the warmth was tempting, but my anxiety drove me on. Quickly, quickly. Bargain for corn and then turn back for home.

Would they still be alive? This thought worried me dreadfully. I tried to push it away by imagining how much corn I could get — I would take a whole sledful home — and by thinking what delicious bread Mama would make with it; just like it used to be, before the war.

I learned a few things during those three days. For the first time I had to rely wholly upon myself, and I lived constantly with the feeling that dangers lurked around every corner. But now I knew I could work out my route quite accurately. I was not afraid of walking through the woods alone, and I had learned how to guess where one could ask for shelter at night and where there was no point in trying. But weakness, hunger, and cold made it ever harder to cope, and I had to say to myself continually, "You must, you must!"

How many kilometers did I put behind me on the third day of my journey? Thirty? More? Again my legs were failing me and my whole body was practically keeling over with exhaustion. I found a large village and hoped I would be able to stay the night there. Then I could start on the last leg of my journey, refreshed, in the morning. Dog-tired and weak with hunger, I looked forward to my night's rest.

But what was that? Loud screams, dogs barking, women crying! Some men had surrounded the village and were shouting and cursing in German. It was strange: I was meeting German soldiers for the first time on my long journey. I had heard that they didn't show themselves much in the villages for fear of the partisans.

When the soldiers saw me they yelled, "Get away from here! Scram!"

Then a woman shouted, "Where do you want to go? You must make a detour round us. We are in quarantine. Typhus has come to our village! You see, they have cut us off. Perhaps they want to burn the lot of us!" She started to cry.

I was stunned. What was I to do now? I had forced myself to the limit already. The village was large; going round it would take at least an hour. And where then? It was twilight. The frost was getting sharper.

I tried to force myself through the human chain of soldiers and others. "Let me through! I don't care. I can't go any further."

Typhus? Typhus? What was that anyway? I had never heard of it. The large village promised warmth and rest. I didn't have the strength to let this dream go. But one of the men grabbed me by the collar and said forcefully, "Where d'you think you're going? Are you crazy? You heard — typhus. You'd be dead by morning. People are dying like flies here. Get out of here while it's not too late, or we won't let you go at all."

He shoved me and my sled far away from the crowds who stood there weeping and moaning.

"Go on, go! Get out!" he bellowed as he saw that I didn't move.

I burst into tears and went. What business was it of theirs what happened to me anyway, I thought. How did they know that I would die of typhus? It was much more likely that I would collapse from tiredness and freeze to death here. Anyway, what did it matter what I died from? Dying of typhus might even be easier; at least I'd be in a house, in the warm.

With thoughts like this spinning through my head I wandered round the village, and with each step I sank deeper into the snow. The moaning and howling of women and children carried to me from the houses.

When I had bypassed the village, I couldn't find the road again. There was nobody there to ask. I was completely alone in that vast expanse.

It grew dark. The snow began to fall in drifts. Everything whirled and swirled around me. I couldn't even see my feet. Where to now? Where was the next village? Was it near? Far? And which direction should I take?

Fear and frustration gripped me. Eventually I couldn't take any more. I sat down on my sled and began to cry. I thought of Mama's words: "You will die, Tanja." Yes, I thought, that is what will happen. No one can help me, and you are far away, Mama. No one will find me here, in this snowbound field.

If only I knew in which direction I should go, I would march on with my remaining strength. But there was no path, only a thick snowy curtain surrounding me and cutting me off from the rest of the world. I couldn't stay sitting there all night; I would freeze. I hadn't died of hunger, but now I would die of cold, like the man I had stumbled upon yesterday by the path through the forest.

I buried my head in my hands, curled myself up as protection against the cold wind that whistled through my whole body, and waited to die. My arms and legs began to go numb. My face was covered with a light crust of ice. My mind became hazy. Soon, soon it would all be over. If only it would be quick.

Suddenly I thought of my family. Back home they would be waiting for me, hoping for corn, counting the minutes. I pulled myself together. While I had the tiniest spark of life left in me, I had to carry on. I must walk on, walk on, regardless where. . . .

I struggled to my feet and stumbled through the white veil of snow and icy wind. Snow and tears stuck my eyelids together. I battled my way forward by guesswork, sometimes sinking up to my belt in a snowdrift, unable to see my hand in front of my eyes. All I could see was a thick wall of snow.

When I had fought my way out of the snowdrifts, it was a struggle to pull the sled behind me. I'll leave it behind, I said to myself. That will be easier. But how would I bring the corn home then? No, I had to take the sled with me.

Gradually the snowstorm blew itself out. Far away in the darkness I made out a dim light. And then another next to it. A village!

I set out toward the lights, floundering and falling in the snow. Then, when I had nearly reached the first of the houses, I suddenly realized that I could not carry on — I couldn't go a single step further. I fell to the ground. Now I was on all fours, crawling. I reached the front steps of a house and heard a dog barking, but I couldn't make it to the door.

I heard voices nearby. "It's another child. It is probably lost. Or the mother froze to death, like that other one recently." It was a young woman's voice.

A different, slightly older voice asked, "Aren't you afraid, Anjuta? Typhus has broken out round here.

Where has the girl come from? After all, they gave orders that no one is allowed out."

"But we must get her warm. We can't turn her away like a stray dog!" answered the first voice.

I wanted to scream, "Please don't turn me away, please don't turn me away!" but instead I felt myself sinking into a deep sleep.

When I woke up, it was already light. I lay wrapped up in a warm fur by a stove. Sunbeams were crowding through the window. "Sun!" I must have said it aloud, because a woman got up from the stove and came over.

"You're alive, my dear. Thank God! We worried about you all night. You were frozen through when we carried you into the house. We thought you were too far gone to live. But what were you doing, all alone at night? You should be glad that the dog started barking, otherwise you'd have died of cold on our doorstep. Now get up and have some hot soup. Then you'll forget all this."

The young woman looked after me. I was happy and looked out at the sunshine, telling myself, "How wonderful it is to see the sun. I haven't seen it for so long. And I am alive!"

I no longer felt the terrible exhaustion of the previous night, and I didn't want to think about all the things I had endured. I ate the tasty barley soup and clung to the thought that the corn-growing regions were already very near.

"The villages with the cornfields aren't far from here," said the older lady, guessing my thoughts. She was also fussing over me. "We go there ourselves, and trade anything that we have in the house for corn. You can reach Oredesch town in an hour. But it's not worth staying there. By evening you'll find the villages where you can barter for grain.

"You have got something to trade?" she asked. "Don't be too hopeful. They are very choosy. You might be lucky, but don't be too quick to give things away. Go from house to house and bargain with people. It could well be that one house will give you more than another. Before the war the farms were in good shape, and some still have food in plenty because they were able to finish the harvest — even if German bombs were dropping all around them. Corn is more expensive than gold, nowadays."

I hurried on. By lunchtime I had gone past Oredesch and had reached a village where I was sure I could get some grain.

It struck me immediately that the people here were wealthy. The houses were new and solid and had obviously been built just before the start of the war. They were made of thick tree trunks and still smelled of pine.

I chose an attractive, large house and knocked at the door.

"Come in, come in," said a man's voice.

I went in and stood still with wonder. The whole room was covered in carpets from floor to ceiling, and it was full of mirrors. I had never seen so many beautiful things in one place before. All my courage left me. Who would be interested in my modest bits and pieces in a house like this?

"All right, what have you got? Come on, let's see," said the man without a word of greeting. In his white linen tunic, unbelted, he looked like a Russian folk hero. Most impressive of all was his thick, well-cared-for beard.

"Well, I" — my tongue wouldn't obey me — "I have come to barter for some grain. I have walked a very long way—"

"Yes, I know," the farmer interrupted. "You want corn, that's obvious, but what have you got to bargain with? Show me."

I opened up my sack.

"No, no, no," he said after he had cast an eye over my pathetic offerings. "We don't need stuff like this. The place is already full to bursting. We can't fit any more in."

"But please, sir," I cried, terrified that he would throw me out at once. "Look at these shoe-soles.

Don't you want these? They are made of real leather and they are brand new." I showed him the soles which the cobbler had given me.

"No, I don't need anything like that," he said quickly. "Hey, Wassili," he shouted through the open door to the next room. "Do you need any soles? There's a girl here, trading."

Wassili came into the room. He was another strong and healthy farmer, but younger. He looked at the soles and turned them over in his hands. "Well, we could give you a loaf of bread for them. If you want a loaf we could do a deal."

Only a loaf of bread? Was it possible? I had pinned my hopes on the leather soles. I had already realized that it would not be easy to trade my other things. But one loaf of bread! I would have to eat it on the way back, and then what would I have to bring home?

"No," I said loudly. "I won't give them to you for one loaf of bread. I need more. My family is waiting for me at home. They are starving."

"More?" The farmer burst out laughing. "You fool, I'm already offering you a good deal. Well, go on then, try and find yourself someone who'll give you more."

I went from house to house. In every one they looked at my bits and pieces, felt the shoe-soles and offered me so little that I went away without trading anything.

Perhaps I must try to bargain with them more? I wondered. But Mama had always said that a well-brought-up young lady doesn't bargain. What was I to do? I couldn't leave the village without any corn.

I knocked on another door. This time I was determined — I would bargain with these people.

An old lady greeted me. "Come in, little one, come in. Oh, my dear, what a long way you've traveled," she said, after I had told her my tearful story. "And now you're to go home with nothing to show for it? Don't look so downcast. My sister and I, we'll help you. It's evening now. Stay the night with us and see what tomorrow will bring. Things always look better in the morning."

When I woke up the next day, the first thing I saw was my sack. It was full of corn.

The ladies said to me, "Little Tanja, we want to give you the grain as a present. We don't need your things. Try to swap them for something else. Perhaps some oilcakes and bran. You can use those to supplement the corn, so that it will last longer.

"There are new rules in our village," they explained. "A new order. The Germans have set up a village leader, a very rich man. People are becoming grudging and mean spirited. But we had put a little corn by and so we can share it with you."

I ran joyfully through the village once more, and was able to trade my soles and other things for oil-cakes and bran.

Now my sled was packed full with corn, just as I had dreamed. The kind ladies gave me something to eat, and slipped me some bread for my journey. They tried to persuade me to stay a little longer and rest, but the thought of home pulled me onward. My anxiety about my family was growing by the hour. I knew they would be waiting for me, worrying and counting the hours and minutes. That very same day I turned for home.

It was the middle of February. The sun was beginning to give some warmth. But the 120 kilometers I had only just traveled now lay ahead of me, and the sled was heavily laden.

So what? I told myself. If I manage thirty to forty kilometers a day, I'll be home in three or four days. I was no longer frightened of the journey. I only worried about my family. Were they still alive? Would I be in time?

Oredesch was soon behind me. The path now led through a field, the same field in which I had endured such torments two days before when I had lost my way. Now the sun was shining and the snow crystals glittered silver and gold like lights on a Christmas tree. It was painful to look at, but the shimmering crystals gave me a good feeling inside.

All at once I heard the snorting of horses and the swish of a sleigh behind me. I hardly had time to spring out of the way before the horses passed me at a wild gallop. They were harnessed to large transport sleighs which were piled high with sacks, and they were storming forward at such a pace that I couldn't make out the faces of the people on board. Nevertheless, my heart leapt with joy because I was seeing *people* in that vast expanse of snow-covered prairie, and I watched them go, wide-eyed.

Suddenly, one of the sleighs was pulled to an abrupt halt. A man wearing a moth-eaten fur cap jumped down, picked me up, baggage and all, and set me on top of the sleigh. Before I could gather my senses he shouted, "Go, Nicolaj! Get going! We'll be left behind!"

Then he turned to me. "Well, little one? Don't you recognize me any more?"

I couldn't believe my eyes. "Uncle Wanja?" I asked.

Iwan Samuilowitsch, as Mama called him, had been a tailor in Wyritza before the war. He had often stayed with us and had even made a stylish frock for my doll. He was always coughing, and Mama said Iwan Samuilowitsch was seriously ill.

"So, you've recognized me after all!" Uncle Wanja stroked my cheek tenderly. "We are taking grain to the partisans, little Tanja, and we have to make sure that we cross this open country as quickly as we can. Once we get to the woods we have the advantage again.

"But what on earth brings you here? Were you looking for food? How could your mama let you go alone? Tell me, Tanja, are you in a bad way at home?"

"Very bad. We are dying of hunger. That's why I came."

"We must all fight and endure, Tanja. Tell your mama. Endure! We will come soon. We will definitely come."

The driver stopped the horses. Iwan Samuilowitsch said, "We can't take you any farther, Tanja. We're branching off here, and your route goes straight on. Take care! Tell them to sit it out back home. We're coming. Be patient."

He shouted the last words when the horses were already galloping. The sleigh drew away very quickly, and I could see it catching up with the line of other sleighs hidden in the woods.

My own path now lay straight through open fields, but I didn't think of the danger. Home! I was going home. I didn't walk — I flew.

* * *

It was the fifth day of my journey. I was nearing familiar surroundings. This day was the most painful. I was very tired, and only one thought kept beating in my head: Are they still alive?

At last I came to Wyritza. I left the field path and turned onto the highway. Should I speak to the people coming toward me along the highway? Perhaps they would know what had happened to my family? No, better not. I don't want to waste a minute.

Finally I reach our gate. I open it with such force that my sled falls into a snow-filled ditch. I don't have the strength left to haul it out. I run along the beaten path and wrench open the door. It is very quiet in the house. . . . My heart stands still.

Mama is standing by the stove with Olja in her arms. She is alive! Mama stammers, "Oh, oh!" She claps her hands together and cries, "Tanja! You're alive! Pjotr! Little Tanja is back again!"

But I hear nothing more. I throw myself into my mother's arms, howling. "Mama, my darling Mama! If you knew what has happened to me!"

Exhausted, I slide to the floor. My mother, weak with hunger, can't hold me.

I manage to say, between sobs, "The sled! The sled, Mama. It's in the ditch. Quickly! That's where you will find the corn."

As Mama rushes out, I sit on the floor with Olja.

My little sister smiles with happiness. She squeezes her thin, hungry body to me and gives me a tender hug.

March 3, 1942. Now it is March already. I am sitting at the window. The sun warms me through the windowpanes. I am writing in my diary, "How I Found the Man in the Snow." Mama is cooking soup with some of the grain I brought.

Papa had thought that barley soup would put him back on his feet.

But Papa died today.

This morning he was ordered to go and see the German Command. Mama went with him because he was very weak. Olja and I stayed home.

It wasn't long before Mama came back. She was beside herself. She said that they had driven her out of the village headquarters because she had made too much noise. Mama told me how the SS-man had accused my father of treason and demanded to know where he had hidden the partisans.

"Father said that was a stupid question," said Mama, "because he has hardly been able to move from his bed for months. But the SS-man bellowed that he was one hundred percent certain that Father was in league with the partisans.

"Father stood as tall as he could and said bravely, 'I

am an honest man and I have never lied in my life. But I can assure you that if I really had hidden the partisans, I would never give away their hiding place.'

"The SS-man went bright red and struck Father in the face and across his swollen fingers. I started screaming, 'Pjotr is my husband! He's not in league with anyone. He's dying. Look at him. He's swollen and bloated. In fact, we're all at the end of our strength!'

"Then they threw me out. It's all over, Tanja. Father will never survive this."

Mama started to sob. "They are killing him. It's all over, all over," she repeated, glancing out of the window. Then she cried, "He's coming," and I ran out into the hall to meet him. But as I was opening the door I already heard the clatter of a falling body.

Father lay facedown on the floor. I wanted to help him up, but he was dead.

Mama cried aloud with grief, "He tripped over the step! If only we didn't have that wretched step!"

But I thought: Papa was determined to come home, and he did it, right up to the threshold. However did he manage it? They had beaten him so badly.

Why have I written all this down? Because it could well be that we will all die like Papa and then nobody will know what we had to suffer. Perhaps one day people who are born later, after the war, will read this. After all, the war must end some time.

March 29, 1942. The Germans have spent quite some time building something on the Siwersker highway, almost opposite our house. At first I didn't know what it was going to be. Now I know. It is a gallows. I had never seen one before, only read about them in books. But the next day there were people hanging high up on the gallows tree, dangling from the crossbar, turning to and fro in the bitter wind. I haven't dared to leave the house for a week. It always seems to me as if the dangling bodies are still alive.

April 10, 1942. Our store of corn has gone. Spring used to be my favorite season, but this spring does not fill me with joy. We are occupied. My father is dead, and we no longer have the tiniest thing to eat. Mama said today, "I am so tired of battling with hunger. I can't go on anymore. I don't have the strength left to fight for our lives."

May 16, 1942. A terrible thing has happened. Starving people are being forced to gather wood and sweep the streets clean. Other, younger ones are being taken to Germany — as captive laborers, they say.

And I, too, am being taken away today.

II. CAPTIVITY

May 16, 1942. "Don't cry, Mama. I'll write to you from Germany. I'll send you lots of letters."

"But will they get through? And will you have a pencil and paper to write with?"

"If not, then I'll write to you in my imagination."

The heavy bolts on the goods train doors clanged across. Everything went dark. Outside we could hear the staccato shouts of the German guards. "Everything fastened? Yes! Ready!"

That's it. Everything is over. Russia has disappeared behind these heavy doors.

Piercing pains in my stomach prevent me getting up. I lie on the floor along with everyone else. What will happen to me now? I grasp a hunk of bread firmly in both hands. A German soldier gave us the bread as we were bundled on board. "Eat it slowly," he warned. "It will have to last you until we reach Germany." As if it could! People have been chewing all around me for ages.

I have to eat it quickly too. I am so hungry. The bread tastes strange. A hint of sawdust, maybe? I know that taste only too well.

The goods train lurches forward. Our journey has begun. I don't really care what happens to me now. My head is spinning; yellow and red dots float in front of my eyes. I fall into a strange doze, neither sleeping nor dreaming.

I wake up when some fresh air blows into the smelly carriage. The doors are standing open, and rays of sunshine dazzle those nearest to them. They are all young girls — but what pale, greenish faces they have. They push their way to the open doors and peer out. I crawl over too, and poke my head into the fresh air. Our long goods train is standing at a crossing by a small station. Men in civilian clothes come over and whisper to one another.

The German guard comes past. "Get back! Back!" He wants us to get away from the door. It's strange; I've eaten up all the bread, but I want more already.

Suddenly, tall women carrying huge baskets appear in front of our carriage. They are pretty, dressed in embroidered frocks and aprons, their hair decorated with colored bands. They look left and right, then take bread from their baskets and throw it toward us.

Inside the carriage, life returns to us. What a miracle! A loaf of bread falls directly into my hands. Then the women disappear from the railway track as swiftly as they came. It really is a miracle. But why were they wearing their traditional dress? What country are we in? Why are the women throwing us bread? How did they know we were coming? Were they waiting for us? And then to disappear so suddenly! They must have been frightened of the German guards. Who were they?

Behind me I hear girls whispering excitedly. "Polish peasant women in traditional costume! They must have dressed like that to show that they would not give in."

That is very brave. They have put themselves in danger for us captive Russians. Thank you, you courageous women.

May 21, 1942. We are taken from the goods train at the station of a large German town. I read "Magdeburg" on the station sign. I have never heard of this place. I try to remember my geography textbook, but I can only think of the names of two towns in Germany, Berlin and Weimar.

We are herded into six rows on the platform. The guards take up positions around us. We hear a command — "Silence! Quick, march!" — and we set off, out of the station.

The line formation begins to spread out a little. My eyes have difficulty adjusting to the bright May sunshine after the long hours spent in darkness.

Despite my weakness, I look at the foreign streets and people curiously. It's strange. Here, it is almost as if nothing had happened in the world outside, as if there were no war. Music is playing. I see many flowers, and women dressed in pretty clothes. One woman is wearing a bright, colorful frock, with a fox fur round her neck. The foxtail swings from side to side as she walks. But why is she wearing fur? It's so warm.

The girls here seem so happy. The boys laugh, without a care. We used to laugh like that too, before the war.

"Faster! Faster!" shouts one of the guards, right in my ear.

We enter a spacious square. A man in civilian clothes stands on a raised platform. He shouts through a loudspeaker, in Russian: "Those who want to work in a factory, stand over to the right. Those who want to work in the fields, stand left."

Everyone is anxious, whispering excitedly. I try to

listen, and mull over the alternatives. One girl says there is more food in the country, so I must try to go there. In any case, at least then I'd see meadows and sunshine. It will be hard work, it's true. But would factory work be any easier?

I go quickly to the left-hand side. The girls who are already there are strong, nearly adult. I look very little in comparison.

Someone gives another order. We are taken to the bathhouse. There is no bath though; it is more like a shower. The Germans — all men! — hose us down row by row, spraying us with some kind of liquid. I have never stood naked in front of a man. What must it be like for the older girls and women! I feel humiliated, for them as well as for me.

We go into a huge building without any windows. It looks like a gigantic barn and it is filled with an array of tables and benches. Everyone sits down. Very tired, I lean my elbows on the table and bury my face in my hands. I would so dearly love something to eat. Perhaps I will never lose this constant feeling of hunger. People are holding whispered conversations on both sides of me, but I don't feel like talking.

Well-dressed men and women come into the hall. They go through the rows and inspect us carefully.

"Get up!" someone yells.

I look round. A girl not far from me stands up. She

is older than I am, and beautiful. Curly golden hair hangs down to her belt and she has deep blue eyes. A fat man with a cigarette hanging from the corner of his mouth has stopped in front of her. He pats her under the chin. Satisfied, he nods and signals that she should follow him.

"The best thing would be to be chosen by a small family firm," says someone behind me.

"Firm" — that is the first time I have heard this word, and I'm not quite sure what it means. But I immediately wish fervently that a family firm will choose me. I lift my head and sit up straight, even if my head constantly droops again with tiredness.

The selection procedure continues for many hours. The rows become emptier. Twice some people come over to me, but then they go on, without a second glance. There are fewer and fewer people in the hall. It's obvious that nobody is interested in me. I try to look wide-awake and keen, hoping to make someone notice. I am afraid that no one will want me and I will have to stay the whole night all alone in this huge barn of a place.

Time goes on. Pressing my face to the table, I no longer think of anything. What will be, will be, I decide. I am feeling ill with hunger again.

At last I and some other girls whom no one wanted are taken from the hall by the guards. We are ordered onto a farm truck. It has no roof and nowhere to sit. It is extremely narrow into the bargain. We stand tightly packed together — that way we won't fall. The truck drives through the town, and again I marvel that it can look so carefree, even festive.

The truck leaves the town and we drive along the highway, a wide and impressive road. Then it turns into a country lane and rumbles between countless fields, trailing clouds of dust behind it. These are the fields where I will be working. How big they are! They seem endless.

It is dark. The truck stops by a field. I can see one isolated house. It is a large, two-story stone building with metal bars on all the windows. My heart beats faster. Where have they brought us? To prison?

Another command: "Take your belongings! Get down!"

I have nothing to take. How could I have, when we swapped everything we once owned for bread? My only possession is an old vest made of rags. I keep it on, even though it is warm here.

I am the last to clamber down from the truck, tired out and covered with dust. The other girls mill about, trying to get the dust off their clothes. I just stare at the iron bars. They make me feel afraid.

You were right, Mama. I won't be able to get hold of paper or a pencil here. So I will "write" you letters, as I promised, in my head. If only you could take me away from here!

Swallowing my dusty tears, I try not to sob aloud. Fearfully, I force myself toward the house with the iron bars.

First we are sent to the inner courtyard. It is large, and there are no guards to be seen. The girls stand by the tap in the middle of the courtyard and wash themselves thoroughly, naked to the waist. I just let the cold water stream briefly over my face, sip some water from my cupped hands and then stand a little to one side.

A sturdy girl with black eyebrows joins me. "I'm called Ljuba. What's your name? I'm from the Ukraine. . . ." She stopped. "But you're crying, little one. Just you stay with me."

Ljuba takes my arm and we climb to the second story. There is a larger room with a stone floor. Iron beds are arranged against the walls. In the middle stands a table surrounded by benches. On the table is some bread, and next to the bread are large clay jugs. The girls sit down on the benches and eat ravenously. Ljuba points to a bed and I reach it with my last strength, falling in a heap and unable to eat even one mouthful of the bread I have taken. I fall asleep instantly.

The morning sun wakes me, shining through the bars. Everyone else is still asleep. I lie there, fully dressed, and beside me is my bread, untouched. I take a bite and chew it blissfully. What wonderful bread! It is almost as good as ours was before the war, soft and delicious.

A gong sounds downstairs. That must be the signal to get up. Yes, everyone gets up from their beds. I feel refreshed; the exhaustion of the previous night is as if it had never been. I wash myself under the tap with the others. Bread and large jugs of milk stand ready on the table. I think to myself, "I won't have to worry about food any more. I made the right decision when I chose to work in the fields."

The truck taking us to work in the fields drives for quite some time. I look behind me and can no longer see the gray house with the iron bars. The girls on the truck with me say that although today the guards woke us at seven, normally we will have to get up at four in the morning and be working in the fields by five.

At last the truck stops. As far as the eye can see there is nothing but endless beanfields. I know it is a bean crop immediately. We sowed beans in the flower beds at school, and I always loved watching the green stems twine their way around the stick supports.

The Master, as he calls himself, is an older man,

not very tall. He says that we must clear away the weeds, and then gives us the hoes in silence.

"Get on with it!" he barks, and we start hoeing. He sits on the verge and watches us work.

The sun is climbing higher in the sky and burns fiercely. I am left behind. The other girls are already far ahead, though they are not hurrying. Now the Master comes over and sends me back to redo the rows I have already hoed. He says I have missed some weeds.

"The roots!" he says. "You must reach the roots!"

I am very tired. I want to ask, "Is it nearly lunchtime?" But I don't dare.

I miss more and more weeds. The Master gets angry and shouts at me. Again I go back and dig out the weeds. What more can I do? I can hardly keep myself upright. The sun beats down mercilessly, and I am covered in sweat.

When will it be lunchtime? And when will this field end? I put up my hand to shield my face from the sun and look into the distance. I get a terrible shock. The field has no end. Soon I will collapse . . . I will collapse, and then what?

The rattling of a cart can be heard in the distance. The Master calls "Lunch break."

Saved. A few minutes to catch my breath, and then it'll be easier.

We sit in a circle. Ljuba pours bean soup into our dishes. The soup smells delicious, but I can only spoon it up and eat it with difficulty. I have to force myself. What is the matter with me? I was desperate to eat before. Ljuba encourages me. "Go on, eat! It's only one o'clock now, but we have to work until six."

Until six! What a dreadful thought. I will never be able to keep going until six. No, I just can't do it.

When I have finished eating, I crawl to a tree by the verge and sit against it. Ljuba sits next to me and gives me advice. "Work steadily, and don't look left or right. That way you won't get left behind."

While Ljuba is speaking I can only think that soon thirty minutes will be over and we will have to start working again, across the beanfield that has no end.

"Get up!" shouts the Master, looking at me.

I must get up, but it's as if I'm stuck to the earth. Nothing can give me comfort here. Everything is alien.

How long will this war go on? Will I live to see the end? And what end will the war have? If Hitler wins, then I will have to stay in these beanfields forever.

"What's the matter?" shouts the Master. "Back to work!"

I stumble back to the bean rows and rip out the remaining weeds. If only six o'clock would come. I can't go on any more. I can't keep my back straight, and my knees are wobbling. If only this field had a boundary, then at least one could grab a few seconds rest before the turn. Perhaps even sit down. But the Master is shouting again. Can't he see that I am nearly falling over, that I feel as if I'm dying?

My mouth is dry. If only I could have a drop of water. Red rings dance in front of my eyes and I can't see things properly. That is why I keep missing the weeds. At last the Master stops sending me back to hoe again. He rips the weeds out himself.

"What is your name?" he asks.

I understand what he is asking me, but my mouth is parched. I have difficulty saying my name.

"Where have you come from?" he continues. "From Leningrad? Ah — a townee. Well, then of course you find the work hard. And you're still quite young. How old are you?"

"Nearly fourteen."

"Hmm. You look younger."

"We starved when your army came," I explain, which probably isn't such a good idea.

"Oh yes," says the Master noncommittally, and then he moves on.

He did say it's nearly time to stop. But when? In one hour? Two? I can't stand another two hours. My hands are shaking — and my back, my back! My body is weak, it is folding together of its own accord. . . . Where can I find some shade?

"Stop!" shouts the Master.

At last. I can see the truck, but how can I reach it? It must look ludicrous — I crawl on all fours and moan softly to myself. Ljuba looks round and turns back. She grasps both my arms and pulls me upright. "What are you doing? They'll send you to work in the town, behind barbed wire!"

Leaning on Ljuba, I stumble forward. She helps me climb into the truck. By now I don't care whether they put me behind barbed wire fences or not.

The days pass. I can hardly eat anything. I can only drink. In the evenings, after six, I collapse onto my bed like a dead thing, a piece of bread in my hand. I chew without tasting. I can hardly get up in the mornings, and I think of the beans with horror. At lunchtime I nod off for a few minutes. At the end of the day, with Ljuba's help, I drag myself back to the truck. And that's how the days go, and they never get better. My second wind never comes.

June 1942. I have worked out that it must be the middle of June by now. Every day I feel worse. I am eating nothing at all now, only drinking. In the evenings I don't wash, and I don't talk with the others.

The Master is not pleased with me. He shouted at me very angrily today, but maybe that will be the end of it.

It is not. Next morning I and two other frail-looking girls are not allowed onto the truck that drives to the beanfield. "You're staying here," we are told. An hour later we are driven to the town in the same truck. Now the factory and barbed wire are waiting for me, just as Ljuba said. Who cares? At least there won't be a beanfield.

June 16, 1942. I am in Magdeburg once more. We are driving down a long, wide avenue, lined with attractive old houses. I read a road sign saying "Broad Street"— I understand both these words. Then the truck turns into a side road, and we come to a stop by a large sign: "Bensch Printers." "Bensch" — that must be the name, but "Printers" — that's a word I don't know.

We are taken into a large workroom. All kinds of parcels and boxes packed with paper and books are standing around the floor. A tall, stern-looking man in a yellow overall comes out of a glass-sided office. He leads me and another girl through the workroom to some tables. He leaves the girl by one of the machines, and takes me farther.

We walk alongside long, narrow tables. Women

are sitting behind them. I can't see their faces — they all have their heads bent, and their hands are sorting something at an incredible speed. Involuntarily I also bend my head and stare at the floor. The man takes me to a spare table.

"Do you speak German?"

"A little," I reply, shyly. I have not spoken aloud for some time.

"Good. Now look," he continues. "There are pictures for children laid out on these tables. Cartoons. You collect the cartoons into batches and place them onto that trolley. Walk up and down the tables, sorting as you go, and make sure you don't miss any. Do you understand?"

I guess what he means, and nod.

The man leaves me to it. I want to look at the work going on around me, and at the women, because I have not yet seen German women close up. I raise my head, and immediately meet the gaze of a young woman. She is very young, maybe only a little older than me, and she has blue eyes. She is smiling at me! Is that possible? A smile in this country! I am pleased and smile back.

The cartoons that I am packing show different kinds of animals. I would like to look at them more closely, but I don't want to be caught not working. So I go up and down, backward and forward. I sort the cartoons into batches, then put them onto the trolleys. When the trolleys are full, they are taken away and brought back empty. After the beanfield, this work seems easy. Very easy, even.

After a few hours I begin to feel dizzy. It is the hunger-sickness again. I am quite used to it by now. I feel sick almost all the time.

The work stops for lunch. A few German workers have gone away; others take thinly sliced pieces of bread spread with something appetizing from their tin lunch boxes. They drink coffee. It smells good. I sit with them, even though I have nothing to eat. Won't they give us lunch here? I can't bring myself to ask. And anyway, whom could I ask?

The girl who smiled at me earlier comes over, points at herself, and says, "Anneliese, Anneliese."

"My name is Tanja," I reply.

Anneliese looks around, slips something under my cartoon pictures, and is gone in a flash. I lift up the sheets of paper. There is a sandwich, filled with plum jam. I stuff it hastily into my mouth, but then I chew it slowly and with relish. It tastes delicious.

After lunch the time goes quickly, but when a bell announces the end of the working day, I feel very tired. Still, twelve hours here in the factory are nothing in comparison with the beanfield.

After work, my group — eighteen women and

young girls — is escorted through the narrow alleys of the town. I look at the street names, and sometimes I am able to understand them. Every house has
a sign on it. "Bakery" — that's a word I know.
"Grocers" — that's more difficult. I must learn more
German, I decide.

At last we come to a broad, attractive river. I hear
someone say "Elbe." I know that name! The German
lady in Wyritza who wanted to teach me her own language mentioned it. I wonder if she guessed what
was in store for me.

High above the Elbe towers a strange building. It
is surrounded by balconies.

"This is the Belvedere," explains the German
woman in charge. "You will be living here. The
ground floor is being renovated, but you will be
housed on the first floor. Careful with the stairs and
the floorboards."

Then she tells us that wake-up time is at six o'clock
in the morning, and that we will leave for work at
seven. In the mornings we will be given tea and
bread. Lunch will be provided at the factory.

"We weren't ready for you today, but tomorrow
you will have something to eat. If you behave well,
you won't do too badly here," says the woman. Then
she locks us in and leaves.

*   *   *

I wake up refreshed the next morning. The sun bathes the whole Belvedere in a bright June light. Now I like the sun again, and I make up a motto to cheer myself up. "The sun shines on everybody, even those who wear the OST badge."

They gave each one of us a badge yesterday evening. It is a square of white cloth, hemmed with blue, and it has the letters OST — "East" — written in large capitals in the center. The badge identifies us as captive workers from Eastern Europe, just as the yellow Star of David identifies Jews. They have ordered us to sew these badges to our clothes. We are not allowed to leave the building without them.

Nevertheless, we can go to and from work unaccompanied. The distance from the factory to the Belvedere is not far. At seven o'clock in the evening we have a roll call, to check that we are all there. The German woman comes to count us and lock us in. After that, we are left alone. It's a pity that we are locked in so early. I have decided that I will go secretly to Broad Street one day. The main street is right by our factory, just around the corner.

Today Anneliese nodded a greeting again. Not far from my picture tables works another German girl, called Inge. She has chestnut-brown hair and dark, intelligent eyes. When she told me her name, she didn't smile.

fully, to avoid being seen. Good heavens! The whole of the first floor is propped up on supports, and the ceiling bulges in places. The whole thing could collapse at any moment. The Belvedere is completely rotten. What a pity. It is such a beautiful building.

I scrub myself carefully with a brush, rubbing until it hurts. The soap won't lather; it's made of clay. I soap myself with it and scrub my whole body again. That stings. I rinse off the soap and pat myself dry with a towel made of sacking. We were each given one of these. I feel better already.

One day last week we were sent home from work an hour early. It was some kind of German holiday. That meant I could go on my long-anticipated excursion to Broad Street. After all, I only had to turn right at the corner rather than left. Broad Street was very near; only a stone's throw away. I covered the OST badge by folding back my jacket and slipped away to the right.

At the corner there was a frustrating delay. A boy of about sixteen came toward me. He wore a brown shirt with the badge of the HJ, the Hitlerjugend — Hitler Youth. I had seen the badge before. Hans always wears one. Hans is a fifteen-year-old boy whom Nowak always calls "numbskull" for some reason, and whom he occasionally cuffs on the head. Sometimes Inge also wears that badge.

Just as I reached the corner of Broad Street, the boy with the HJ badge waved a collecting-tin under my nose and demanded an "offering" for the front. We had each been given three marks at the end of the month, as "wages." Now I held the money tight in my hand, and I had no intention of giving it up for the German front.

"I don't have any money," I said, trying to hide my accent. Then I ran on.

People were shaking these tins up and down the street. Women and children called out, "For the front, for the front!" It seemed very strange to me.

"Well, thank goodness," I said to myself, at least I've got past them. I walked cautiously down the length of Broad Street.

I passed shops containing fashionable clothes, but they didn't interest me and I didn't stop to look in the windows once. It was the food shops that fascinated me, but I didn't dare to go too close.

All at once I saw a beautiful girl painted life-size on a poster. The girl was dancing on a flight of steps and underneath was written, "Marika Rokk in her new film."

How pretty she is, I thought longingly. And what a long time it is since I last went to the cinema. When would it have been? Before the war, of course.

I went nearer to the box office. I would so love to

see beautiful, graceful Marika Rokk dance. And then? Then I'd see what happened.

"Do you want to go in?" asked the cashier.

"Yes, yes," I mumbled, holding out the coins.

My hand trembled. I had to muster all my courage to stop myself from running away while the cashier gave me the change. For a few seconds I stood as if on hot coals.

Everything went smoothly. I was in the cinema. The auditorium was practically empty, but the lovely girl danced and sang on the screen. I forgot everything. Then the film stars started to speak, but of course I couldn't understand them.

Overwhelmed by the dancing and the music, I came out of the small cinema and went down Broad Street in the direction of the Belvedere.

I had nearly reached the corner when I suddenly saw a policeman, or to be more accurate, I realized that we were heading straight for each other. The policeman was wearing a green uniform and cap and holding a short, thick, rubber truncheon in his hand. He paced slowly and purposefully, gazing over everybody's heads.

My blood ran cold. Where could I hide? There was no cover.

Too late. We were directly opposite each other, and there was nobody between us. How frightening the policemen in Germany are! Just their faces are enough to make you die of fright. I thought he'd realize straight away that I am not a German. "Where is your OST badge?" he'd say. And "Where are you going, and why so late?" All these thoughts flew through my head. They terrified me. I'll end up in a concentration camp, I thought. I'll definitely end up in a camp. What wouldn't I have given to make myself invisible, so that I would not be discovered. I let my head hang lower and lower. . . .

Just a few more meters. Soon he would say "Stop!"

To my amazement he said nothing. I raised my eyes and saw that the policeman was looking in the opposite direction. A group of rowdy young people on the other side of the road had attracted his attention. Safe! I really was born under a lucky star. You often used to say that, Mama.

I speeded up a little, turned into the side street, and ran as fast as I could to the safety of the Belvedere.

In the Belvedere they were drinking tea, or, more likely, hot water. I sat down with them. The roll call had not yet been called because of the holiday, and nobody had noticed my absence. I was still so shaken by my brush with the policeman that I couldn't wait to get to bed, but it took me a long time to get to sleep. I lay awake and daydreamed that the war will soon be over and that I can go back to school, and that, if I learn to dance, perhaps I can become an actress like Marika Rokk.

October 1942. Four months have passed since they took me away from home. Now it is autumn. The year 1942 is coming to its close. I don't know what has happened to you, dear Mama. Of the two slices of bread that I get daily, I put one aside and dry it out by the window of the Belvedere. Perhaps I will be able to send you this dry bread. I know you won't have bread at home. I don't dare think about whether you are still alive.

We have heard nothing about what is happening on the eastern front. The woman in the bed next to mine says, "I am giving up hope that our lives will ever return to what they were before." Nobody around me has faith in the future. Everyone is scared of something and we all live in fear, even the Germans themselves.

We are all fed up with the meals in the factory. We are given soup twice a day, but it is only hot water with a couple of pieces of turnip and sometimes a small potato swimming in it. In addition we get two slices of bread and margarine, but never more than a thimbleful. The margarine smells of candle and the bread of sawdust. After my experience of famine, that doesn't matter much to me, but the girls from more prosperous areas can't bear it.

Today they moaned more than ever. It's autumn, so there should be plenty of vegetables, but there are none in our watery soup.

The German woman who gives us the food said, "I have nothing to do with it; go and see the foreman."

"Who is he?" I asked. "Where will I find him?"

"Upstairs, on the fourth floor," came the reply.

Without more ado I took my bowl with the watery soup and went up to the fourth floor. Without even knocking I pulled open the door marked "Foreman" and went inside.

"Here," I said, plonking my bowl on the table. "Try our vegetable soup. Could *you* eat it?"

The foreman, a stout, elderly man, breathing asthmatically, opened his eyes wide and looked astonished. It was only then that I realized I must have lost my mind, to storm in uninvited like that. I was sure to regret it.

Shocked back to sanity I stammered, "I'm sorry, I'm sorry. . . . We are all so unhappy, and it's better, isn't it, if we are all content?"

The foreman burst out laughing.

"Of course," he said, "it's much better if everyone

is content. But is it really possible to keep everyone happy, Miss?"

I stayed silent and thought, He's laughing, and he doesn't look angry, but who knows.

"What's your name?" asked the foreman. "Tanja? Well, Tanja, you are brave and you speak German. What do you do in our factory? Sort pictures? Aha. So, our vegetable soup doesn't come up to scratch? Unfortunately, I can't do anything about that; the soup comes from a central kitchen for East European workers. Still, I'll ask whether we would be allowed to cook your meals ourselves in future, in our own kitchen.

"It's remarkable," he continued. "You are so small but already brave."

"I get that from Mama," I replied.

"Who is your mama?"

"Nobody special. Just a Russian woman," I said. "But she was always brave, and when my sister and I were dying of hunger she went out to the woods at night in order to find something to eat. The patrol forbade it during the day."

"What sort of patrol?"

"The German one, of course."

The foreman thought hard.

"Listen, Tanja, I'll see what I can do, even though

I'm not really responsible for you Russian workers. I am only responsible for the German workers in our factory. But I would like to help you. Come to my house after work. I live on the way to the Belvedere. Here is my address: the street and house number." Then he added quietly, "Only promise me that you won't tell anyone about this."

I hid the piece of paper in my hand and went downstairs. The lunchbreak was over and I had not had a single spoonful of soup — I had left my bowl with the foreman by mistake.

When I came out of the factory it was still light, and the rays of the setting sun lit up the walls of the houses. It made me dizzy. Should I go to the foreman's house or not? I debated with myself for a while, but hunger drove me onward.

I found the right street and house quite quickly. It wasn't large, as it happened, although it did have three stories. In places the plaster was peeling from the walls. I looked at the names displayed by the entrance. The foreman lived on the third floor, at the top of the house. There was no lift, so I climbed up the stairs. I wondered how the foreman coped, considering his asthma.

I rang the bell. An elderly lady opened the door. She smiled at me in welcome, as if I was an old friend.

"Tanja? Yes, I know. My husband has already told me about you. Come inside."

I was amazed when I went in. I had expected well-furnished rooms, but what I saw was very different: poky rooms, small and whitewashed, without any wallpaper on the walls. Against the living room wall stood a sideboard, with two photographs displayed upon it. I noticed those immediately. Well, I thought, the Germans obviously don't all live in such luxury after all.

"I am Frau Meier," said the elderly lady. "You must be hungry, Tanja. Sit down and have something to eat."

Frau Meier gave me a salami sandwich and a large mug of milky coffee.

Mmm! I savoured the aroma greedily. I hadn't smelt that for quite some time. The salami didn't just smell good, it tasted wonderful. I drank the coffee and felt very content.

Now Frau Meier didn't seem as old as I had at first thought. She sat opposite me and watched me eat. "You poor child," she said, tears trickling down her cheeks. "I have children myself. Two boys. And they are both on the eastern front."

"They are killing our soldiers," I wanted to reply, but I kept quiet. Why say that? It wasn't Frau Meier's fault.

Then she showed me the photographs of her sons. Two young men in uniform looked out at me.

"Stefan is twenty-two and Peter is only twenty," said Frau Meier. She got up and fetched a dictionary from the bookshelf. She pointed out particular words in the dictionary as she spoke. "We didn't have children until we were quite old, Tanja. My husband was a typesetter. For a long while we were unable to have children. It was a hard time for us. And now they are far away, outside Stalingrad."

Frau Meier took me to see a map which took up practically the whole wall of another room. She indicated with her finger. "This is Stalingrad, on the Volga."

Did that mean that the black tanks had already got as far as the Volga? The thought shocked me.

"Where is Magdeburg?" I asked.

"Magdeburg? Here it is."

I took a deep breath. Even on the map, the distance between Stalingrad and Magdeburg was immense.

"I know what you are thinking, Tanja." Frau Meier shook her head. "But the war will not go well for the Germans. . . . God will punish us."

"God?" I asked. "You believe in God?"

"Yes, Tanja, I still believe in him, and I hope that he will help my children to survive. And you, do you believe in God?"

"I . . . No. I believe in" — I riffled through the dictionary, unable to find the right word — "in conscience."

"In conscience?" said Frau Meier, startled. "You are right. Conscience should dictate one's life."

"That's what my mama says."

"I know that there are many good people in your country," Frau Meier continued. "Perhaps they would help my sons if ever —"

Who would help them when they have invaded a foreign country and are destroying it! That was my first reaction. But I thought better of it and said, "Frau Meier, I am sure this is an anxious time for you."

The foreman came in breathing heavily and gave me a little package. "Here, Tanja. I have found some sausage for you. But don't tell anyone. That would be dangerous for us both. Come to see us every week if you can. I will help you."

I went back to the Belvedere and thought, all women around the world worry about their children. So why does one country ever invade another? I just can't forget the black tanks, emblazoned with swastikas, which appeared that day on the Siwersker highway, and also the columns of wounded prisoners of war. At the time, Mama, you said, "So much blood, so much blood. Those poor boys . . . their unhappy mothers." But whose fault is it that sons are killed and mothers weep? Whose fault is it? Not Frau Meier's, I'm certain of that. But whose? Is it only and entirely Hitler's fault?

The more I see of the daily lives of people in the town, the more obvious it is that they are not as happy and carefree as they seemed at first. When I watch the passersby, I see that many of them look sad. Recently they have started to look anxious and uncertain, too. That is something I didn't see before.

On the streets they are rattling their collecting-tins more and more energetically: "For the front! For the front! For our soldiers!" and on the way to work I see more and more posters saying "10,000 marks for the traitor's head." The people they are looking for have probably escaped from a prison camp or evaded conscription. The women gather in front of these posters, shake their heads, and go off in silence.

There are also more soldiers on the streets. I have had to stop my little excursions to Broad Street, and I seldom dare to visit the foreman's house. In the evenings we are forbidden to put the lights on in the Belvedere, so we go to bed early. We don't have any books or a radio. In fact we are almost living like animals; twelve hours working in the factory, then sleep. Eating enough to stay alive, and trying not to think of anything else. But sometimes I do think, especially when for once my head is not spinning with hunger. Lying on our beds in the darkness we whisper about things that we would not dare to say out loud. What can be going on back home, on the Russian front? But no one has any news. We are cut off from the world to which we belong, and the world that surrounds us is alien.

January 4, 1943. Sleet is falling. The town grows dark and the Belvedere stands on the steep riverbank like a fairy-tale castle made of glass, shrouded in fog and silence.

Sometimes we feel as if the ceiling is about to fall on our heads. The Belvedere is decaying, the supports on the ground floor are rotted through. The building work has already been abandoned. But despite the danger, it is not a bad place to live. I love the view of the Elbe. When I look at the river through the large windows of the Belvedere, I think of our Oredesch. Then my spirits revive and the depression lifts.

The Belvedere has another advantage. Nobody except the captive workers lives there. In the evening the Germans do the roll call, lock the door, and leave us alone until morning. That gives us a feeling of freedom such as we had long forgotten. Since we were transported we have had no say in anything, neither in our lives nor over our possessions.

I remember how that German soldier burst into our house and shouted, "Matka, Matka, walenki dawai, russki winter, russki maros!" And then he pulled your fur-lined boots off, Mama — yours, of all people. It was no use you saying that we were lost without your boots; that we children would die of starvation because you wouldn't be able to walk to the village in order to bargain for bread. You begged him and cried, but he didn't care. He said that he was the master now.

It is just the same here. They have the power and we are helpless. They can forbid us to leave the house, can change the work we do without consulting us, feed us when and how they like, or just send us to the labor camp. I am beginning to get used to this "discipline"; I have fewer and fewer hopes and dreams.

It is good that the Meiers still help me when I pluck up courage to visit. What would I do without them! Dear Frau Meier is friendly to me, gives me food and coffee, and even some sausage every time I leave. This little package gets smaller each time, however.

The last time I went to the foreman's apartment Frau Meier was crying bitterly.

"Oh, Tanja, my eldest has been killed in the siege of Stalingrad, and my younger son is seriously wounded," she said, and hugged me to her breast. She wants me to comfort her. Me! Somehow this good woman sees me as a strange link between herself and her sons, even though they are soldiers fighting against my people. That fact is something that doesn't occur to her. She thinks that if her sons are fighting in my country, that is something that binds us all together. She said it herself: "Tanja, when I see you I feel as if my sons are with me. You must come and see us more often." I couldn't really understand this, but I tried hard to comfort her.

On that particular day I sat with her for a long time, but the foreman didn't come and didn't come. When he eventually arrived he looked very gloomy. Because of his sons, I assumed. But then he said, "Tanja, you Ost-workers will soon be taken away from our business and sent to work in various munitions factories around Magdeburg. There are hard times ahead of you, little one, and I don't know whether you will be able to carry on coming to see us. If you are allowed to leave the barracks, do come to us. But not a word to anyone." He put a finger on his lips.

This time, when we said good-bye, he gave me a larger package to take home: "In case we don't see each other again. . . ."

January 27, 1943. One day last week we were told to pack our things. We were going to be taken to work somewhere else. They didn't tell us where, of course.

Nowak called me over to his glass-sided office. "I am sorry for you, girl," he began hesitatingly. "The work that is waiting for you will be hard. Life in general is becoming harder. I will also have to go to the front now."

On the same day a young woman came over to me. We had hardly ever spoken to each other, but she had often looked in my direction. She was almost as small in build as I was, and she had a tired face like an old lady. Once she had brought me a piece of bread and butter. The slice of bread was small and spread very thinly.

"Everything is rationed," she had apologized. "And I have four children and my husband is at the front." Then she swiftly moved away from my table.

This time, when she looked around and made certain that everyone was occupied and no one was watching, she came across to me carrying a cardboard box. She slipped it quickly under the table and said, "Tanja, in the box is a pink dress with white dots. It should fit. There is also a pair of shoes. Yours are worn through, I can see. I can't give you a coat, because I have altered everything to fit the children.

But it is already winter and it can be very cold in the factories, so I have put a warm cardigan in."

At the end of work that day I said good-bye to everybody. Everyone in my group knew that I was being taken to a labor camp, and I got the feeling that they were watching me with pity. I went to Inge; her table was next to mine. Inge nodded and even smiled a little, for the very first time. Hans said good-bye curtly, without even raising his head. Anneliese gave me a friendly smile, as always.

I found it hard to tear myself away from my cartoons. I had learned to speak German quite fluently from looking at the pictures and their captions, as well as the street signs.

When we reached the Belvedere in order to pick up our things, I broke down and started to cry. The unknown life ahead of me made me afraid. But I am grateful to the Belvedere. In the seven months I spent there I was able to regain some strength and recover a little.

We are driven through the whole town. Everyone clutches their bundle or suitcase. I have wedged the cardboard box containing the shoes I was given and the pink dress with the white dots under my arm. I am wearing my vest and the old cardigan, and I have bound a towel around my head, but it is so cold and the wind blows so fiercely that I can't stop shivering from head to toe. It is drizzling, half spring rain and half slushy snow. Head down, I make myself as small as possible so that the snow and wind don't whip against my face.

We have been traveling for more than an hour already. At last, when it is already starting to become dusk, we arrive outside the town. Several rows of barracks are standing on a large, empty expanse, bounded by a double row of high barbed-wire fencing. A guard meets us. He is wearing a black uniform and holding a fierce-looking dog on a leash. The entrance is thrown open and we are allowed through. Our escort, an older German from the factory, has given the guard a piece of paper. The guard counts us and says, "Twelve. That's right."

We stand close together, in a pitiful heap. Then the guard takes us to one of the barracks. In it stand twelve empty beds.

"You will get up at half past four in the morning," says the guard. "Then you will be given some food. At five o'clock you will form orderly lines and march six kilometers to the factory. The early shift begins at six o'clock in the morning, the late shift at six o'clock in the evening. You will only go to work in marching order. You are forbidden to leave the camp except in your marching columns. The OST badge must be worn in a visible position. The stove" — he points to a small, round stove in the middle of the room — "may only be lit once permission has been given. Cooking on it is forbidden. If anybody breaks the camp rules, he or she will be punished and sent to a concentration camp."

The guard rattles this off. With a "Heil Hitler!" he leaves the barracks.

The January wind has chilled me to the bone on the way to the camp, so I lie down on the lowest bunk of a three-tier wooden bunk bed and wrap myself in a coarse gray blanket. Then I notice a girl's head above me, watching me intently.

"I'm Nina," she says.

"Tanja," I answer. "I come from near Stalingrad. And you?"

"Me too. Do you know Sluditzy?"

"Sluditzy? I had to go through Sluditzy in the winter of '41. I was looking for corn. I nearly froze to death there."

"Franzusowa is my surname," Nina goes on. "Perhaps you have heard it before?"

"No, never. But it is an unusual name: Franzusowa. You don't look like a French girl. One can tell you are a Russian immediately — gray eyes and a cauliflower nose!"

Nina is not offended. She just grins.

I like Nina Franzusowa immediately. As I fall asleep I am pleased that I have found a new friend.

I must have been sleeping so deeply that I missed the wake-up call of the guards. Nina wakes me up. "Come on, Tanja!"

Next to the beds stand jugs of hot water, and small bits of bread are laid out on trays. We soon finish eating and go outside to form our marching columns. It takes a while until everything is sorted out. We are counted many times. In the darkness the guards scream: "Halt! Right turn! Move!" The dogs bark viciously.

I shiver from top to bottom. My naked feet in their wooden clogs are particularly cold. I am saving the shoes and the dress with the white dots. I will put them on when the war is over.

At last the marching columns start to move. We walk for a long way through the streets of the sleeping city. The trampling of hundreds of wooden clogs on concrete and stone rings in our ears. When we reach the factory — a huge, sinister-looking building — there is still not even a glimmer of daylight.

We are taken to the factory floor. Here milling machines and lathes screech and shrill. I put my hands over my ears. The manager leads me to one of these machines.

"Here," he says. "You stand here and stick the iron bars into this opening. Then you turn the wheel and the process starts. The machine is off at the moment. Now I press this button and it's on. Understood?"

I guess rather than understand what he means, but I nod my head anyway: understood, understood. I have probably been worrying about nothing; it's all quite simple. I press the button. What is going on? The machine isn't running. The wheel isn't turning. I put my ear to it and listen, but there is so much noise in the room that I can't hear whether the wheel is turning or not. Perhaps I can feel it with my finger.

"Oooowww!" My scream resounds through the entire hall. I snatch back my hand: A flap of skin is swinging from my finger and blood is flowing down my arm. I howl with pain and shock.

The manager comes running over.

"What's going on!" he shouts. "By thunder! What an idiot! Why did you stick your finger in the machine?"

"I thought the wheel wasn't turning . . ."

The manager swears, then gives me a rag and growls, "Here, bind it up." I bandage my finger.

Now I have to sweep up the rubbish, because that can be done with only one hand. I am pleased because

I don't have to work very hard all day. But the manager threatens me furiously, "You'd better not be faking!"

The next day I am moved to a different milling machine. Here I have to push pieces of metal into an iron drum. The machine does everything on its own. You just push things in and then place the round finished pieces into a box. The machine sprays out oil, and after an hour I am covered with oil from head to foot. The manager is dissatisfied. "Watch what you're doing. You have to achieve the set target," he shouts.

I don't get near the target all week. The twelve hours in this factory seem to last a terribly long time. I have constant headaches just from the noise. But here there is no Master Nowak and his tablets.

After work, when it is already completely dark again, I trudge back in my column, without looking right or left. If only we were at the barracks already.

In the evening I line up for vegetable soup. It is even worse here. Hunger is plaguing me again.

My store of sausage was quickly used up. I shared it with Nina, who screwed up her eyes with satisfaction. In the evenings, after the soup, we throw ourselves onto our pallets in order to gather strength for the next day.

Now the night shift is coming closer. Perhaps the

night shift will be better. Maybe I could run away from the camp in daylight and go to the foreman to get some sausage. He did promise me. . . .

But the night shift turns out to be a complete nightmare. I can just last out from six o'clock in the evening to two o'clock in the morning, but then I practically collapse from tiredness onto the milling machine. That would be something, if the cogs got caught in my hair! I am completely covered in oil and cry every night. A mixture of tears and machine oil covers my face. I wipe it with my arm, but that is also oily. I talk to myself in whispers, "Hang on a little longer, just a little. Soon the morning will come, then things will be easier."

At last the week's night shift is over. I can breathe again. Even though the twelve-hour day shift is hard, it is nothing in comparison with the night shift.

Hunger torments me terribly, but it is impossible to slip out and visit the foreman. We are allowed to leave the camp for two hours a week, but I would not make it there and back in that short a time.

It is still very cold. Sleet falls constantly. I wrap myself up in everything that I have. Today I have come back from work in a dreadful state, shivering. I lie down on my pallet. Nina gives me her coat. It doesn't help.

"You have a high fever," she says.

That's the last thing I need! What will happen to me if I am ill?

I can feel my senses failing. Red circles are swimming toward me. Where are they taking me? Mama, oh Mama, where will I end up?

February 1943. I open my eyes. I am lying all alone in a light room. Someone in a white coat says in German: "You have survived the worst, but you are still very weak. You were going to be taken from the medical unit back to the barracks today, but I will give you two more days convalescence. Make sure that you get your strength back quickly, though. We don't want sick people here."

Nina comes and supports me. I feel completely limp, and can hardly put one foot in front of the other.

"How long have I been ill?"

"Two weeks," answers Nina. "I wanted to visit, but they wouldn't let me near you. At first they said you were hovering between life and death, and then that you would die. It's rare for someone to come back to the barracks from the medical unit. But now everything will be better, you'll see. It is February. Soon it will be spring."

I breathe the fresh air in through my nose — and

it's true, it does smell of spring. I love spring so much. I can always feel it coming a long way ahead.

"Oh, it's wonderful to be alive when the spring starts," I say to Nina. She drags me along with difficulty, because I am leaning practically my whole weight on her arms. Then she sets me down carefully on the bedstead, holds out a piece of bread, and hands me some herbal tea.

I gaze out of the window and think again how wonderful it is to be alive. Good will surely win over evil. We must make it through to the end of the war at all costs, because it must end sometime and then we will be free.

March 1943. Now the sun is really warm. Nina and I have stayed a little behind the marching column. We are not far from the camp. As usual, I am using a piece of sacking towel as a scarf. I have shown Nina how one can hide the OST sign behind it. Then I notice that someone is following us: Some boys of about seventeen are catching up to us.

"Are you Russian?" they ask.

We are suspicious and frightened. These Germans are speaking to us captive laborers openly on the street — that hasn't happened before. We don't understand what they want from us.

"You needn't be afraid of us," says one in a low voice. "The Nazis are nearly finished, but we are not Nazis. The German army was decimated at Stalingrad."

I stand as if rooted to the spot and my mouth drops open. Nina glances distrustfully at the boys.

"Yes, it's true," says another. "Hitler is nearly finished; the Nazis are finished. We are fighting against the Nazis."

I can't believe my ears. To hear "Hitler is nearly finished" being said openly on the street, instead of the usual "Heil Hitler"! Can it be true? We would have liked to talk to the boys and inquire a little further. Instead I stand dumb, tremble with fear, and look around timidly. Nina is also trembling. Then she tugs at my arm and we run like crazy, without looking behind us, into the camp.

It is only then that we calm down and whisper together on our straw pallets.

"Yes," I say. "I believe them, and what they are saying is sure to be true. Otherwise they would have told the camp leaders that we were not displaying our OST badges."

"There are probably more like them," comments Nina, and I agree.

"We'll have to find them again," I decide.

Now, whenever we are coming back from work we

position ourselves at the end of the marching column and look around carefully at the spot where they spoke to us. But it is all for nothing — they don't come near us again. What has happened? Have they been sent to the front? To a prison camp? It is very dangerous to talk like that around here. And we are hearing this kind of talk for the first time, now in spring 1943.

April 1943. The night shifts are pure torture for me. Not a night goes by in which I don't cry. And every night I think of you, Mama, and try to write you letters in my mind. They help me a great deal. When I "write" to you it immediately makes me feel better, however badly the day has gone.

I rarely achieve the target. The manager bellows, "You should be sent to a concentration camp for your miserable amount of work!" But that wouldn't be a solution for the manager, either. Many workstations are not occupied. Yesterday a young German of seventeen worked next to me. Today he is not there any more. The manager said, "He has gone to the front." I see neither young nor old men working at the factory. Women take their places, and other foreign workers.

This munitions factory isn't like Bensch Printers. Even the people are different here: morose and really unpleasant, some of them. I try to ignore it all. Sometimes, in daylight, I manage to let my thoughts wander. But when I work at night I only think of one thing: "Don't fall asleep whatever happens."

If the German army has been wiped out at Stalingrad, that would mean that our soldiers have succeeded in turning back the black tanks. This thought brings hope. But at three o'clock in the morning my head sinks onto the workbench of its own accord. I stop thinking, and I don't care what the manager will do to me. But he has seen me already. He sees that tears are running down my face. At last he says angrily, "Take a break! Go and have a nap in the crates."

I disappear instantly. The crates, full of assorted junk and dirty rags with which the machines are cleaned, stand at the back in a corner of the hall. I rummage around in one of them and curl myself up like a hedgehog. I float away. Something red, bloody and whistling comes swimming toward me. At last I fall headlong into an abyss. . . .

"Get going!" shouts the manager into my ear.

Is the break over already? It only seems to have lasted a second. The manager looks at me so strangely; he doesn't even shout at me. With an effort I put one foot in front of the other. My legs have gone to sleep because of their cramped position. No, it's better not to sleep at all, I tell myself. But the next night everything repeats itself. There is nothing I can do about it. I can't go on like this. Why didn't I freeze that time in the wood? Why didn't I die in the Belvedere? I'm at the end of my tether. I have no strength left with which to fight for my life — not even now, when rumor has it that our troops have won the battle of Stalingrad.

Nina reckons that our life is not very different from that in the concentration camps. But I'm sure it's much worse there. One morning it bucketed down with rain, and so we marched quicker than usual. My blanket was wet through. I always wear that blanket now; during the day it serves as a coat, and at night I cover myself up with it.

It was nearly day, but a dull half-light because of the rain. As we went along beside a high wall — amazing, really, that I hadn't noticed it before — we had to stop suddenly. Some of our marching columns had already gone past, but my column came to an abrupt halt. Police guards had formed a cordon in front of us.

We heard dogs barking and loud shouts. Women in black uniforms had taken position in front of the guards. I looked at them. They were tall, blue-eyed, blond — really attractive women. But their voices were sharp. "Go, go!" they yelled. Hearing them yelling "Go" sent shivers down my spine. I heard the girls in our row whispering, "Those are the famous Aryan women."

Together with the police, the women in black formed an almost impenetrable wall. But despite this I did see something. Between the gaps I could see people in striped clothing. They went quickly, bent over, with their heads hanging low, and they had a yellow — no, even green — skin color. One man (it might even have been a woman, I couldn't tell) hung back a little, and immediately truncheon blows rained down onto his head. The unlucky man shielded his head with his arms, but the blows came still more heavily. He went faster, stumbling, but the blows hit him again and again. It hurt me. It hurt me as if I were being beaten myself.

One last command, then the beautiful women in black turned around sharply, following the captives, and vanished with them behind an iron door.

It was clear to me that I had just seen part of a concentration camp. But what are Aryan women exactly, I wondered, pulling the drenched blanket more tightly around me. Is it the name of a particular race, or is that what they call the guards in the concentration camps?

That evening, as I was standing in line for the vegetable soup, I was still thinking about the concentration camp and became so lost in my thoughts that I didn't notice the gap widening between me and the person in front. A guard pushed me roughly into position. Suddenly, feelings of protest and outrage rose up in me, triggered by the thought of the people in the striped clothes, and I screamed, "Don't be so brutal," straight into the guard's face.

"What!" he bellowed. "I'll show you what brutal means!"

In the same moment I received a blow that sent me flying against the opposite wall, my bowl and lid shattering against the other side. The guard struck me again and again, screeching, "You Russian pig!"

Somehow I pulled myself together and stood upright, as the camp rules demanded. My neck burned with pain, my lips were bloody, and the blood dripped into the palms of my hands. I stood there and swallowed my tears. Nina calmed me down. "Count yourself lucky. They could send you to a concentration camp for that."

Now I lie on my straw pallet and think about all this. I imagine that Germany is a huge metal press, like the one that stands in the corner of the factory where I work. When this press descends onto a piece of iron, it presses it together until it is quite flat and nothing remains of its original shape.

May 1943. All around our East European women's camp, other camps are spread out. A little further along the street is the French camp, and right next to us lies the camp for Poles, both only for men. I have not yet been able to find a camp designated for Russian men.

When Nina and I are overcome with hunger, and if we manage to get out, we walk over to the Polish camp in order to find bread. I don't dare go to the French camp, somehow.

The Poles are usually kind to us. They probably pity Nina and me. Whenever we come, someone always calls: "There are the Russian girls. We must help them!" and they bring everything they have, refusing to take money for it, even though we offer it to them proudly. We are ashamed to beg. It is different when I say, "I would like to buy some bread."

Nina and I are very grateful to them. They remind me of the Polish women who threw bread into our train carriage when we were brought to Germany.

It is easier to bear hunger in the summer. The vegetables help. If Nina and I manage to lag behind our column a little, I quickly dart across to the market stalls displaying cabbages or carrots, and say, trying to sound as German as possible, "A cabbage, please."

The German market vendors don't always notice that I am a Russian, and then they are pleased to sell.

But sometimes they say, "You are Russian. You can't buy. That's not allowed." Or sometimes just, "Go away." In short, no two Germans are the same. Even so, we are all well supplied with cabbage because most of the vendors want to get rid of their vegetables, so they just look around briefly and stuff our coins into their apron pockets. The camp leaders don't like to see our stocks of cabbage, but mostly they pretend not to notice. That is why we all chew cabbage in our camp. Sometimes we try to cook it on our round stoves, but if the guards see that they knock the cooking pots off the stove with sticks and everything pours out all over the floor.

July 1943. I lie on my bed and keep my eyes closed. That way I can think up my letter more easily. Today I don't want to imagine one that is as sad as the last time.

Every Sunday someone in the barracks has been playing the harmonica. Today you could hear it again, and I went to have a look. Two Frenchmen were playing and a few couples were dancing. Others had come along and were standing around the dancers. There were Belgians, Poles, and Frenchmen. The Frenchmen and Belgians come from other camps nearby. There are absolutely no girls in their camps, unlike ours, where there are only girls. Also, they are allowed to walk around freely, whereas we are very rarely allowed out of the camp.

I have always loved to dance, but this time I just sighed and turned back to the exit. Then a pair of eyes met me: such dark, large eyes! They were obviously looking only at me. As I left the barracks, I could still feel those eyes.

A young man caught up with me and said, "Mademoiselle . . ."

How strange this word sounded in the camp! But I recognized it.

"Mademoiselle," he repeated. "Vous êtes Russe?"

"Ja, Russin, Russin." I guessed what he wanted to know.

"Honoré," he said, and laid his hand on his breast at the same time.

"You are called Honoré!" I said. "And I am Tatjana." I told him my full Christian name, just as one should.

"Tatjana, Tatjana — charmant!" cried Honoré.

I understood. He liked my name.

Honoré knew a few words of German. I on the other hand knew only two French words: "merci" and "monsieur." But with the help of eyes and hands we were soon able to make ourselves understood. I gathered from his story that he had been brought here two months ago from France. Also to work in

Germany, naturally. He was eighteen. "And you?" I showed him with my fingers. Sixteen. (Well, nearly.)

Honoré is an attractive young man, average height, with an unruly head of hair and lovely eyes. When I looked at him closely, I noticed that he squinted a little with one eye, but it hardly shows. He seems so thoughtful and kind and looks at me so nicely. No one has ever looked at me like that before. My heart was warmed by his gaze.

We went along the main road through the camp together. It was nearly curfew time. Honoré said, "I will come again tomorrow, ça va?" and took my hand.

"Ssawa, ssawa," I murmured, without knowing what it meant. Then I suddenly tore myself away from his hand and fled into the barracks without looking back.

When I came back from work today, I swallowed the vegetable soup quickly and started looking for a mirror. Nina doesn't have one either. Someone gave me a broken piece, and I stared curiously at my mirror image. A thin, very pale face looked at me. The blond, wavy hair was hanging down lankly, the gray-blue eyes looked serious, yet a very tiny smile lurked behind them. Did he really like me? I looked at my appearance disbelievingly and very critically.

I combed my hair with a broken bit of comb. Then I was ready to meet Honoré.

He came at half past eight, as he had promised. We still had an hour and a half until curfew.

"Let's go out of the camp," suggested Honoré.

"We can try," I agreed.

Honoré walked on the side where the guardhouse stands. I hid myself behind him. The guard watched us through the window, but when he saw the Frenchman he turned away.

The camp is surrounded by fallow land, and a not very deep ditch goes through the middle. The ditch was dry. We sat on the edge and let our legs swing. The sun was sinking slowly toward the horizon. It was a beautiful large orb. Everything around us was tinged red with its light. It also gave Honoré's face a reddish shimmer.

"Lovely," I said, indicating our surroundings with my hand.

Honoré repeated, "Yes, lovely."

And then suddenly he started to sing: "Chantez, chantez pour moi . . ."

It is a familiar melody. It's a pity that I couldn't understand the words. Then he looked at me and sang another song: "Je t'aime, je t'aime, c'est tout . . ."

His voice is not very strong, but it has a nice sound. Honoré sang one song after the other. In comparison with the dry, curt German of the guards, the French seemed like music. I couldn't take my eyes off

Honoré, and the sound of the words "Je t'aime" was so good to my ears that I immediately felt inspired to learn French.

Then I came back to reality. "Quickly, we must get back to the camp, Honoré!"

We jumped up and ran. The guard threatened us with his finger, but he left it at that. At the turning into the barracks I waved at Honoré. He was still standing at the gate.

August 1943. Last week I had night shift and we didn't see each other for the whole week. The shift was a nightmare again. Again I cried every night.

Now today it is Sunday. I have slept well and wait impatiently for Honoré. We have hardly reached our ditch before I ask, "Schontee, schontee." I know by now that that means "sing." And Honoré sings for me all evening. Again I learn a few French words, in particular those which come into the songs and which I like because they sound so lovely: "Jamais," "mon amour," "ma chère."

When Honoré sings "Je t'aime," his lovely eyes look sadly into mine. I have now completely given up learning German. When I come back from work I just don't feel like reading notices, and the Germans don't talk when they are working.

Later on, as I lie next to Nina, I whisper a few

French words to her. She likes hearing them. Soon I will be able to talk to Honoré in French.

September 1943. The summer has gone by so quickly. Autumn arrived along with the rain, and I shivered in my jacket. When Honoré saw that, he said decidedly, "We must buy you a coat immediately." He swapped his few wages and the next packet from home for a coat, and then he gave it to me happily and proudly. The minute I put it on I stopped shivering.

Once, when a pipe burst and the whole of the front of the camp was under water, Honoré went knee-deep into the water without a moment's hesitation and carried me across in his arms. I feel embarrassed when he makes such a fuss of me, particularly in front of other people. But he doesn't care: Honoré is a real gentleman. He calls me "petite Tatjana."

December 1943. The year 1943 is coming to an end. Now the town is being bombed more and more heavily. When the bombs fall nearby, we leave our workstations and run to the administration block. They have made a bunker for East European laborers in the cellar there. I hardly have time to lay my cheek against the bench before I fall asleep and don't care about anything.

During the day I can't usually sleep after an air-raid warning. I chat with the other girls and learn French. The time flies, and I remember that I have only completed five years at school. What would I do without Honoré! He has made my life here much easier. I couldn't bear this kind of existence without him. No, I couldn't bear it.

July 1944. The town is being bombed almost daily. When we go through the town after a raid we see ruins everywhere. I have to think of those young men who said, "Hitler will soon be finished." Now it really does look as if they were right.

Honoré always comes to our meetings looking cheerful, even though we can only rarely see each other.

Once he came along, gave me a packet of bread and sugar and said, "Here, for you from Maman." And then he whispered in my ear, "Tatjana, the Russians have gone on the offensive and the Americans are bombing the whole of Germany. The war will soon be over." Then, without any warning, he burst out, "I love you, Tatjana, mon amour, mon amour. . . . And you, Tatjana, do you love me too?" He waited anxiously for my answer.

I had to think about it. When people love each other, they kiss, but Honoré and I have not yet kissed each other. In fact, I have never kissed anybody. Does that mean I don't love him? But what about his songs? I would find it hard to live without them any more.

"I think I love you too."

"And will you come with me to France?" asked Honoré. "I have already written to Maman, saying that I won't be coming back alone."

"Honoré," I interrupted. "I must go home when the war is over. It could be that my mother is still alive."

"All right," agreed Honoré. "First we'll find your mother, and then we'll travel to my home. After all, I can't speak Russian, but you can already speak quite good French. You won't have any problems."

His arguments sounded convincing. However, I stayed silent, because I didn't know what to say. I didn't want to pretend to Honoré. Whenever I am alone again I can only think of our house and you, Mama, and sometimes it seems to me that my desire to learn might not just be a daydream. But no, when the war is over, everything will have been destroyed. I will be nearly grown up and will have to earn money in order to keep us all.

November 1944. The town is now being bombed night and day. The air-raid sirens are continuous, and although we are pleased because we can rest a little and every bomb attack brings the hour of freedom a little nearer, it is still frightening. The sirens have hardly begun before we start to panic.

This time it is particularly bad. In the cellar everything starts to rock and the light goes out. The noise of the falling bombs is unbearable. It feels as if our eardrums are going to burst. I fall to the floor and roll under the table.

And then everything does come crashing down above us. It's a miracle that the ceiling holds.

When we climb out of the cellar, the factory is unrecognizable. Everything is in ruins. Not one building has been left standing; that's how accurately the bombs have been targeted. The hidden iron girders — the last things that remain of the factory — look like gigantic prehistoric monsters.

I go along the street with Nina. Almost all the buildings have collapsed. Some of the houses had been damaged before, and large mounds of roof tiles were piled up nearby. This time bombs have fallen onto the tiles and blown them to rubble and dust.

A soldier is standing in the middle of the road, leaning on his bicycle. His uniform is dirty — I have never seen that on a German before. When we go past him he sees the OST badge on our clothes and says, "Well, girls, this is it. I have come from the front. Everyone is panicking, and now I can see why.

Germany is falling apart. Hitler is finished. The Nazis are going to pieces. The whole of Europe must hate Germany so much."

We stand and look at the heaps of rubble and dust with him. He seems to expect pity, but we can't feel any pity for him, even though we can hear so much suffering in his voice, so much frustration.

When we finally get to the camp, chaos reigns. We all have to line up. The police divide us up according to new lists and then make it known that this camp is shut and we will all be given new work. We will move to a new camp today. Nina and I are on different lists. That hurts me very much and we both cry for a long time.

Guarded by two police guards and with a small group of girls and older women — eleven people in all — I go back into the center of town. Not everything has yet been destroyed here. The American bombers find it difficult to get to the town through the blanket fire of the German antiaircraft guns.

We are housed in a six-story building, right at the top, under the roof, and we are to work on the ground floor. Work benches have been brought here from the ruined factories. They say that this used to be a chocolate factory — it really does smell of chocolate — but now it will be a small munitions factory. We are given a lot more freedom and can go into the town. But the town hardly exists any more. It lies there like a dead giant, and inspires us with dread. With one siren after another wailing, we don't want to go out anyway.

Here I get to know another girl, Tamara. Tamara is two years older than I am. She will soon be eighteen.

One evening after work, Honoré suddenly appears. "Honoré!" I am so pleased to see him. "How did you find me?"

"I can always find you, Tatjana," says Honoré. "Always."

We haven't seen each other for a long time because of the bomb attack, and I hadn't been able to tell him where we were being taken, because I didn't know myself. And now he had miraculously found me!

Honoré is very down. I notice that at once. He says, "Tatjana, I am being taken to work digging graves. I think we are going West, toward our frontier. Perhaps I can flee to France. But what will I do without you? Promise me that you will wait for me. Promise me. I will find you, wherever you go, if I don't die in the meantime. Give me your word that you will wait for me."

Honoré's eyes are full of tears. It hurts unbearably to look into his kind, loving eyes.

"Honoré," I say, "I will try to wait for you. But

you can see what's happening here yourself. I could easily be killed in all this devastation. We must say good-bye." I kiss him for the first time.

The girls are all standing around us, but we cry and kiss each other without noticing them and without being ashamed of our tears.

Honoré has to make an effort to tear himself away. He turns around again and again, stands still and waves. I can't bear it, and I run away to my bed and weep.

Tonight the sirens started for the fourth time. Air attack! For the fourth time everyone ran to the cellar clutching their things — everyone except me. When I made it back to the sixth floor after the third alarm, I threw myself onto my mattress and went to sleep, hoping that the night would soon be over. The town is seldom bombed in the mornings.

And now the wailing of the sirens has begun again. I can hear all the mattresses squeaking together as the girls get up and run past me. Half-asleep they knock against my own mattress, which stands by the corridor. The last girl — Tamara — bellows in my ear: "Get up! Quick! Alarm!"

I am in only my underwear, so I pull the rough blanket from off the bed and wrap it around me. When I get to the cellar, I cover my ears with my hands to shut out the fearsome sound of the airplanes. A moment later there is the most incredible noise. I think the earth must be breaking apart. The lights go out, and then the whole world crashes down around my head.

Then there is silence. I try reaching out with my hands, but I can only feel rubble. It is pitch-black.

"Tamara!" I cry. "Are you still alive?"

"Yes, yes." I can hear her muffled voice answer me. "I'm here, I'm alive, but we are probably buried under the debris."

We sit there for what feels like an eternity. Then we hear men's voices in the distance. All at once a beam of light cuts through the darkness.

"Is there anybody there?"

"Yes, yes!" we shout desperately.

They pull us out, one after another, through a narrow opening. It is a rescue team that has found us. They are three Germans, no longer in their first youth, all wearing helmets. They are peasants, by the look of them. The faces under the helmets look tired and strained.

I gaze around me. Fires are burning fiercely every way I look. The wind that fans the flames is strong enough to knock you over. Six floors have collapsed on top of our cellar. The box containing my dress and shoes must be a write-off. By some miracle the bricks have fallen in such a way that the small cellar window wasn't blocked. If they hadn't, we would now be lying buried under that mountain of brick and slates.

In the meantime the sun has started to rise, but the sky stays threateningly dark. An unbroken ring of fire surrounds us. We are trapped, eleven Russian girls and three Germans wearing helmets.

The Germans look for a way through the flames, and we follow them. We dash from one street to another, but the toppled walls block our path again and again.

Somehow we manage to leave the flames behind. We run out of the town. The fires blaze to our left; to our right the dawn is breaking. We run across wasteland, through craters. We go in silence. What we have suffered in the last few hours has drained us of our strength, so that we can't even rejoice properly about our escape.

I run barefoot over the clammy, cold earth and try not to lose sight of our rescuers. At the same time I wonder what made these Germans, who have brought so much death to our country, put their own lives in danger in order to save ours? They knew from the beginning that there were only Russians in that cellar. No one except East European laborers have lived in that abandoned house for ages. What kind of people are they, these three? Whoever they are, they are not fascists, that is certain, and I will always remember them with gratitude.

December 1944. When it is light, our rescuers drop us off at a new camp. This camp is many times bigger than ours was, but now it is bursting at the seams. There are so many people crammed in here, all wearing OST badges, that one can hardly find a spare centimeter of ground. It looks as if they want to gather all the East European laborers into one place. But why? Various rumors are flying around. Some say it is in order to shoot us; others claim we are going to be swapped for prisoners of war.

Tamara and I don't know what to do. The barracks are overcrowded, and we have not been told where to go. At first we stand out in the open. Then we find a place sheltered by the barracks. We lean against a wall, shuddering with cold. How could I have been so stupid not to take the box and my things into the cellar with me? Now I am left without a winter coat and without clothes. The war is nearly over — everyone talks about that quite openly in the camp — but the pink dress with the white dots which I saved for so long lies buried beneath the rubble.

Some unknown girls bring me a pair of old clogs from the barracks, and Tamara rummages in her bag and gives me an old shirt. I will use the shirt as a blouse, and we are going to try to make a kind of long sleeveless smock out of the blanket. But it is not that easy to find a pair of scissors, a needle, and some thread. We cut out the blanket on an old plank of wood. We have only just finished one side before there is another air-raid warning.

"Let's run away, Tamara," I say. "We can't stay here."

We run helter-skelter out into the open field.

Great swarms of airplanes appear in the sky, coming straight in our direction. We are running toward them. As the planes thunder above our heads, we throw ourselves to the ground. Then, all at once, it gets really dark. The planes are blocking out the sky and the sun — the whole world.

We are lying in a shallow ditch about three kilometers away from the camp. The air-raid alarm has stopped.

"Tamara," I say. "Look! Rain is falling over the town."

"What do you mean, rain?" answers Tamara. "Those are falling bombs."

"Bombs?" I say in amazement. "But it looks like rain. Watch . . ."

"There are just so many of them. Unimaginably many."

Bombs falling like rain? A shower of bombs? I can't calm down.

After about a quarter of an hour, the planes turn back, but a thick pall of smoke hangs over the town. We go back to the camp. The camp hasn't been hit, but nobody seems to be bothering about us. We don't get anything to eat, and still no one knows where we will sleep tonight.

We are hardly back in the camp before the alarm goes off again. Again we flee, but the planes are already very near. I see a bunker intended for the Germans. We are forbidden to go in there. I grab Tamara by the arm. "Come on!" She hesitates, but the planes are already overhead. We dodge into the German bunker.

No one takes any notice of us. The bunker is occupied only by German women holding small children in their arms. We hear a shrill whistling that freezes our bones to the marrow, and then a terrible crash, as if the earth is exploding.

The young women opposite us press their little ones to their breasts. These German women are also so scared that their eyes are nearly popping out of their heads. The children cry heartbreakingly. Now it's the Germans' turn. It is only a just exchange for their own bombs, but that's not the point. I feel sorry for the children.

The sirens send out the all clear. We climb out of the bunker. Everything else has been destroyed, but our camp is still standing. That is remarkable in itself.

"Tamara," I say. "We can't stay in this town. Look, there is only rubble and broken slates left, and even that is still being bombed. Come on, let's run away into the countryside. There's nothing to bomb there, and we can wait there for the end of the war."

"What about the concentration camps? Have you forgotten? Running away means the concentration camps," Tamara reminds me.

"There won't be any concentration camps left by now," I say confidently. "You can see all the chaos for yourself. Our camp isn't even guarded any more. Let's set off now. Tonight they will bomb us again."

Before we start, we finish off our sewing. The needle and thread has been hanging off my smock all this time. We don't dare to throw away the camp badges yet. Tamara takes off her OST badge and puts it and her ID card inside her bra. I have a few German marks which I hide in the same way, just in case. That is all quickly done, and then we run to the station.

The station platforms and waiting rooms are bursting with people. The whole place is filled with an incredible noise. Where shall we travel to? In which direction? We can't ask anybody; that would be too dangerous.

The things that are going on in the station are un-believable. The Germans have always seemed so disci-plined before, but here everything is in disorder: people are screaming; children wail. And not a single police-man anywhere. That's quite something. But we must hurry. Most importantly, we must get some tickets.

Tamara leaves everything to me. She sits down on the arm of a bench — so that I don't lose her, she says. I run to the ticket office. It isn't easy to get to the front as everyone is pushing.

When I get closer to the ticket office, I notice to my horror that the Germans push some kind of card through the ticket slot before getting their tickets, and the ticket seller only gives out the tickets once he has checked the card. Now what? Our German money isn't going to help us after all. What about showing our ID cards? No, that won't work. If we do that, we'll not only not get the tickets, we'll be handed over to the police into the bargain! I have wasted all this time for nothing. I fight my way out of the mass of people. I decide not to say anything to Tamara for a while; otherwise she might run straight back to the camp. I must think of something else — and quickly.

I push through to the platform. It is chaotic here, too. A passenger train is standing there and everyone is boarding it, but I don't dare to ask where it is going. The Germans have strange trains: every carriage has its own door. The Germans sit down, and I see that nobody — imagine it — nobody has asked them for tickets! I decide that we don't need tickets, and run back to Tamara.

"Come quickly!"

"Have you got them?" She is glad.

"We'll travel without tickets! Why should we waste our money when we might need it later!"

We walk onto the platform and squeeze ourselves into a carriage. Behind us, the people who can't fit on are objecting strongly. There aren't any spare seats, so we squat down in the aisle. A few children are crouching next to us, holding a large dog. I like dogs, but I don't feel very confident about this one — it is growling quietly.

The carriage is intended for eight people, but twenty people have already squeezed themselves in. And then the suitcases, the bags, the rucksacks . . .

The Germans' clothes are as ragged as ours. With any luck that will make us less conspicuous.

It's obvious that the Germans are also fleeing, but where to? We sit as still as mice and hardly dare to breathe. If they were to find out who we really are!

At last the train starts to move. I sigh with relief. Let's get out of this hellhole! The train goes quickly, and I urge it on silently. Let's just get out of Magdeburg.

I notice that a lady is looking at us suspiciously. She turns to me and ask, "Are you from Magdeburg?"

I nod. "Yes, yes, from Magdeburg."

I manage to say it without any kind of accent. She wants to ask more, but I close my eyes as if I am tired.

The tension grows. The dog growls. Perhaps he senses that we are not German. How long have we been traveling? Two hours perhaps? Not far enough, but time is getting on. I squeeze Tamara's hand. That is our signal. We get up and shove ourselves forward. I look through the carriage window. There are only fields — no towns to be seen. That's very good. At the next station we push our way to the door through the rucksacks and suitcases, and jump onto the platform.

Whew! Saved! At least for the time being. We look around. It's only a small station, so the town won't be particularly big either. Perfect.

Feeling like an older sister, I take Tamara's hand and lead her across the empty platform to the exit. But a man in uniform is standing at the point where the platform meets the station area, and he is checking the tickets. As quick as a flash I turn back, dragging Tamara along behind me. She pulls against me. "What's the matter?"

"Ticket inspector, that's what," I say. "We'll have to find another way out."

But all around us is a solid, heavy fence, without a gap anywhere. You can usually guarantee that all fences will have a break in them somewhere — but not German fences. We can't follow the railway track either; we would be noticed immediately. "If only I hadn't listened to you and had stayed in that other place! Now we'll definitely be sent to a concentration camp," moaned Tamara.

"You and your concentration camp!" I burst out. "We will just have to think of something."

But however much I try, I can't think of anything.

We are leaning against the wall by the exit. The ticket collector is standing just around the corner. How are we going to get past him? I poke my head around the wall. On the other side of the station building I can see a square. That means freedom. And it's only about fifteen strides away. But the ticket collector is as sharp as a guard dog. He clips the tickets of the few passengers with lightning speed. I observe all this minutely. The more I watch, the more I realize how utterly impossible it will be to get past him unnoticed. Only a miracle can save us now! With dwindling hope, I look out on to the empty platform, now spattered with the first raindrops.

A train comes in and waits for a short while. A large group of Germans carrying suitcases and bundles get off. A man in railway uniform goes ahead of them. He strides swiftly toward the ticket collector and says confidently, "These are refugees. You must let them through. They don't all have tickets as they are only passing through, but they will buy tickets at this station. There are twenty-two in all."

Without hesitation, I pull Tamara along behind me and mingle with the group of German refugees who can go through the barrier without tickets.

"Eighteen . . . nineteen . . ." counts the ticket collector.

My stomach ties itself in knots. Now we are in the station building, and there is the exit to the square already. Behind me I hear, "Twenty-two? There are more than that here."

"Please," says a woman's voice nervously. "Look, here is my passport . . ."

I don't stay to hear anymore. We leap down the last of the steps leading into the town. I am completely shattered and my legs won't carry me any farther. This time it's Tamara who drags me onward. "Come quickly, or they might still catch us."

I let myself be pulled along, though I don't believe that anyone will run after us. There are so many refugees now, German refugees. That means that our soldiers are already in Germany. So we will soon really, truly be free.

When we have left the station behind us, we tear

up our camp passes. We don't need them anymore. We must keep our OST badges, though. They are the only things that prove who and what we are. Now we must think up a cover story.

We are already outside the town, tramping along a dirty, rain-sodden path that leads across a large field. "Perhaps our story could be something like this," I wonder aloud. "We are East European laborers who worked in a city — let's say, Berlin. We were going to be taken to dig graves — Honoré had to do that, after all — but our transport was bombed on the way, somewhere in a big forest."

"There isn't much forest left in Germany," Tamara interrupts.

"That's true. Well, whatever, let's say that it was a forest anyway. The bombardment stopped, we saw the dead around us, were frightened, and ran off. We got lost in the forest, walked farther and farther, and suddenly found ourselves here."

I have no idea how far Berlin is from here, or even whether it's the west or east side of Germany, but Tamara says the story sounds quite plausible.

In the meantime it has started to get dark. At last a village appears in the distance.

"That's where we'll go," I suggest.

"And quickly, because I'm starving," answers Tamara.

Fear had made me forget my hunger, yet we haven't had so much as a crumb all day. When I think about it, my head spins.

We are approaching a large farm. It is so large that I get nervous, and Tamara's hand is also trembling in mine. The farmyard is paved with stone. On the left-hand side it is roofed over, and cows and horses stand beneath. A two-story stone farmhouse rises up at the end of the yard. Grand steps lead up to the entrance.

We stand dithering at the farmyard gate and don't know how to call the farmer. At last somebody sticks his head out of the window. Then a young man appears on the steps.

"What do you want?" he asks curtly.

"We would like to work for you, in return for our keep. We wouldn't expect any money," I explain.

"Work for your keep?" After thinking about it for a while he asks, "Where are you from?"

"From Schleswig-Holstein." This strange name which I heard on the train simply pops into my head.

"From Schleswig-Holstein?" he repeats, disbelievingly. "And what will you do? Can you milk cows?"

"Cows? Not really, but we can learn fast," I assure him.

"Hm." The man thinks about it, scratching his back as he does so.

Secretly I plead with him. Please, say yes. We are so hungry we will soon fall over. Do say yes!

But the young man says, "No, we don't need you. We can manage by ourselves. You are very weak. There's no point."

Bitterly disappointed, we trudge on to the next farm. We go through the whole village, knocking at large and small houses. "Please let us work for you."

"What can you do?"

"Anything. We'll do anything you say, but please take us on. Pay? We don't want pay. We would be satisfied with some bread and hot water. . . . Do take us."

"No," comes the reply everywhere. "We can manage on our own. We don't have any food to give away." They look at us more and more suspiciously.

"I can't go any further," says Tamara, almost too quiet to hear. "I am so hungry."

"Me too," I groan. "We should at least ask for a piece of bread."

"Do you really think they'd give us any?" says Tamara.

Night falls. Weak and hungry, we sit against a fence and shiver with cold.

And now what?

"We must go to the police," says Tamara, as if she is answering my unspoken question.

"No, wait. Let's think about it first." I try to convince her.

But I don't have any idea what to do. It is already dark. Where shall we stay overnight? Outside? If we did that we'd be taken into custody as tramps, and that would be the end of our flight to freedom.

We are in a very sorry state, and so tired that we don't care much about anything anymore.

We sit leaning against the fence for quite a while. Suddenly I hear voices and footsteps. A group of people carrying bundles and rucksacks is passing on the road.

The people sit down in no particular order, not far from us. The whole thing reminds me of a gypsy camp, but it is not a particularly happy gathering. A man speaks loudly in German. "You will soon be found shelter. You will stay the night in this village, and be given something to eat. Tomorrow morning we will continue our journey."

I pull Tamara to her feet. "Come on!"

"What's the matter?" she asks, bewildered.

"Quickly," I say.

We mingle with the crowd of refugees. Soon we are also found shelter. We are taken to a house without being asked for any identification. The man who brought us says to the hosts, "These are refugees.

They are very tired. Give them something to eat and somewhere to sleep. That's an order from the mayor!"

We are staying with elderly people. We can see that they are poor. The little room is very sparsely furnished. There is a table covered with a gray waxed cloth, and very dim lighting. Our escort leaves again, and the old people ask us to sit down at the table. They go to and fro, spreading the table with sausage, bread, butter, and milk. We chew in silence, frightened of questions. Luckily, our hosts aren't talkative. They ask nothing. I rejoice inside: Who knows what tomorrow will bring, but today we are feasting! Tamara must feel the same, but we are so nervous that we don't even dare to look at each other.

The old folk lead us into a second room, just as small. This is obviously their bedroom. In it there stands only one large, broad bed. We lie down on it and sink deep into the featherbeds. Featherbeds above us and underneath us! What a luxury to sleep in German featherbeds after three years on a hard straw pallet.

In the morning, I am woken up by loud voices. I recognize the voice of the man who escorted the refugees yesterday. His voice sounds angry.

"Who are these people with you? Judging by the list, there are two too many."

The old people mumble some kind of answer, shocked. We must get up. Our hosts look at us expectantly. I feel ashamed of our deception, but I simply tell the man, "We are Russians. We met your people by chance. But we are also in need, because our train was bombed."

He stands there as if struck by lightning. Without saying a word, he takes us to the village leader, the mayor of the surrounding area.

And there we sit, half-dead with fear, in the hall of the village leader. He is not at home. We wait. At last he arrives. He is not tall, but stocky, with protruding eyes. His striped vest stretches tightly across his stomach.

I repeat everything that I have already told the old people.

The village leader stares at me and says, "Hm. Where was your train coming from?"

"We were working in a factory in Berlin, and the factory was bombed."

"What kind of factory? What was it called?"

"I can't remember. I lost my memory after the dreadful bomb attack. It is already much better, but I just can't remember the name of the factory."

"And this one? Has she also lost her memory?" He nods his head in Tamara's direction.

Tamara sits there, expressionless, and although she understands a little German, she pretends not to have understood, and says, "Not understand. Not understand."

The round eyes of the village leader get wider and wider. Our story is very flimsy. He's not the only one to think so; I do, too. But we shiver so much and must look so frightened, pitiful, and unhappy that after a few more questions and unhelpful answers he waves us away resignedly and picks up the telephone.

Now he must be ringing the police in town. Again and again he tries to explain to someone that the "East European laborers" are actually only two girls aged sixteen and eighteen, that they represent no threat, and that he is willing to take responsibility for them.

The conversation progresses slowly. The village leader wipes sweat from his face. After numerous telephone calls he is allowed to keep one of the girls with him, and to send the other to the village inn-keeper.

The mayor could quite easily have gone through the official channels. If he had . . . but he didn't. So we owe him a lot, I decide, while he scribbles notes on a piece of paper.

They keep me in the village leader's house, and Tamara goes to the inn.

"My wife has not been able to get up for two years," says the village leader. "She is very ill."

It's true; I can see that she is very ill. She is pale, with sunken cheeks, and her hands are only skin and bone. She says quietly, "It's good that you are staying with us. You can help Eva with the housework. Eva is our daughter. She is in the middle of her exams at the moment and has a lot to do."

I am amazed by this woman's eyes. They are marked by pain, but still so blue. Kind eyes.

Eva comes in. She is eighteen. She looks down at me. She is blond and also has blue eyes, but her gaze is without warmth.

Now I am a housemaid. It is my duty to keep the house tidy and do the washing. The cooking is done by Eva's grandmother, Frau Klose. She lives some-where in the neighborhood and comes every day. She doesn't talk much, but I get on with her well. Just as for Frau Meier before, I am not a "laborer" for her; not a "Russki" — the Germans usually say these words disdainfully — and also not just a drudge, but simply an "unlucky scrap" that was taken from her home very young. That's why I don't know anything practical, she believes. And so, with German thoroughness, Oma starts to teach me things.

"You must always turn socks inside out before washing them, then rinse them well and allow them to dry on the wrong side. However, the whites must be dried right side out — it's more hygienic."

I wash Eva's undershirts and socks without much enthusiasm, but I notice that Frau Klose is right, and I agree with her that what she is teaching me will one day come in handy.

When Frau Klose comes in, she always greets me with "Good Morning." Only Eva says "Heil Hitler" or sometimes doesn't greet me at all. She and I have no contact with one another. It doesn't matter anyway, I decide. Apart from her I am not doing badly in this house.

Tamara is made to work harder. She has to wash mountains of dishes. She stands in the kitchen from morning to late evening, and so we only rarely see each other, even though we live very close. She does get very good food, though. I don't get as much, but I can't really complain. Pea soup, two or three slices of bread a day, usually spread with plum jam. But there is something the matter with me; I could eat constantly.

The bread is kept in the kitchen cupboard. It has often already been cut. The torment it gives me when I come into the kitchen to sweep! For three days I have managed to control myself, but the bread lies there quite openly. That means that they trust me; that's why they don't lock it away.

I battle with myself for a few more days, but then the temptation becomes too great. In an unguarded moment, when nobody other than the invalid is in the house, I cut myself a cobweb-thin slice of bread. I tremble and don't cut it cleanly. That gives me a big shock and I try to make it better. Even worse!

I squash the bread together in my hand and run into the barn. There I stuff it all into my mouth at once, and then chew slowly and with relish. Now I do this every day. Afterward I chide myself: They are trusting you. And you? You are just a thief!

Then one day the bread is gone from the kitchen cupboard. But nobody says a word to me about it. Thank goodness they've taken it away, I think, very relieved.

April 1945. Many months have passed. Spring is just beginning and the sun shines more strongly. I sit in front of the house and have the joyful feeling that things are soon going to change. German refugees are passing along the street in a constant stream, carrying rucksacks, bundles, crying children — just as we did when the Germans were advancing. Eva goes around in a filthy mood, won't look at me, and even shouts at her parents.

All at once a whole host of young, tall men in German army uniform come running into the courtyard.

They rush to the water hydrant and spray water onto their dusty, tired faces and drink greedily.

To my great astonishment, I hear that they are talking Russian.

"Who are you?" I ask curiously.

"We? No idea who we are now," answers one. "And you, you must be a Russian girl?"

"Yes."

"Well, then you'll be going home soon. The war is nearly over. Hitler has fought his last battle, and those who took his side made a big mistake."

"And what about you, did you fight for Hitler?"

"Looks like it."

"And now what will happen to you?"

"What will happen? Prison . . . or, if we're lucky, we can stay on the run in a strange country."

Suddenly they all start speaking at once, and I understand. They are all Russians, Hungarians, Romanians — but they fought in Hitler's army and betrayed their own countries.

"It's a shame that you were on Hitler's side," I say. "Such decent-looking men . . ."

Their tired faces flicker in something like a smile.

"Oh, my dear," says one. "If only we could turn the clock back. It's a lost cause, setting yourself against your own people. Now no one wants us any more, neither our own folk nor the Germans. And all because we didn't recognize what an evil cause we were serving."

"What are you talking about?" someone else interrupts angrily. "You wanted a better life, preferably soon. And for that you'd have been prepared to fight for the devil himself!"

"Stop arguing. Hurry up." Several voices break into the quarrel. "The Yanks are on our heels."

I watch as they continue to argue on their way down the road, arms waving. They disappear into the distance, and I watch them go. What will happen to them now?

Then another troop of soldiers comes running into the yard. This time they are real Germans. They are dirty and tired. They start to wash at the hydrant — and brush their teeth!

What are they doing, wasting time? I wonder. They have got the Americans on their heels.

When the soldiers leave again, Eva comes running out of the house. She shouts after them. "Traitors! Cowards! You won't protect us? You surrender? Then I will defend Berlin, all on my own!"

Her father comes running and leads her back into the house. She is in hysterics. From all this I can see more clearly that the end of my captivity is near.

III. FREEDOM

April 1945. The next day, the Americans drive into the village in their jeeps, without firing a single shot. Huge trucks full of soldiers drive past, and a few jeeps stop in the yard.

The village leader told me the previous evening that as far as he was concerned the war was over, and that Tamara and I were now free. He said that for the time being I could sleep in the attic as before, but he would not give me any food — he doesn't know himself how they will manage now.

Is the war really over or not? I can't say for certain. Tamara and I pass the time doing nothing. Nobody takes any notice of us. We are completely free — so free that we have not eaten at all today. There is no way of getting any food. All the shops are closed.

The Germans have hidden themselves away in their houses and have pulled the curtains tightly closed. I try to find out who is in charge of the Americans, but that turns out to be quite hard. I don't know a single word of American English. I don't even know what rank their badges signify. So I can't find out whether the war is over or not, and — most importantly — how we are going to get home.

The Americans lounge casually on cigarette crates and chew something. I go over to them and say that I am a Russian girl, but they stare over my head and don't hear me out, shrugging their shoulders. "Don't understand."

I don't give up, but try again. "Russian. We are Russian."

They sit in groups, look into space, chew and chew and murmur, "Yeah, yeah."

"I need to eat. Eat, eat."

"Yeah, yeah," they repeat.

In my frustration, I run to the attic and rummage for my OST badge — here in the village we didn't have to put it on. I hold it to my dress, against my chest, and tap my finger on it.

"Aha." The Americans begin to nod. "Okay, okay!"

I like the sound of this new American word, even though I have no idea what it means. I repeat it happily. Then I point to my mouth, make chewing movements, and say, "I want to eat, okay!"

"Yeah, yeah," says a tall, stout man, and he goes to his jeep and fetches a box of chocolate bars.

"Okay?" he asks.

"Yes, this is okay," I answer and fall upon the chocolate.

I had long forgotten how good chocolate tastes. Tamara comes running and we start to wolf down one bar after another.

The American who brought us the chocolate taps himself on the chest. "John."

"You are called John?" I guess.

John takes a small English-Russian dictionary from his huge trouser pocket. He leafs through it for a long time. Then he says, "Russki karascho — I love Russki. I see Russki soldier on the Elbe."

Now I take the dictionary and show John the words, "Thank you. Amerikanski also karascho."

May 1945. Some days later, Tamara and I come to a decision. It is about time we went into the town to find out if the war is over and we can go home. We can't find that out here in the village. The Americans shrug their shoulders. There are no Germans to be seen on the streets.

I say good-bye to the invalid wife of the village

leader — the poor thing is lying there quite alone — and tack the OST badge on to my dress again. Tamara does the same. We take each other's hand and stroll down the country road and into the town.

"What date is it today?" I ask Tamara.

"The eighth or ninth of May, I'm not sure exactly. Why?" she replies.

"Because I was brought to Germany at the beginning of May. That is almost exactly three years ago. . . ."

"Except that now we are completely free again, Tanja. We don't always want to think about the past. That is gone forever. It is better to rejoice in the present."

All of sudden we both want to shout, to sing, to dance. But imagine, Mama! We couldn't remember a single song all the way through to the end!

"Fine," I said. "Then we'll just sing them all as far as we can."

I enjoy the singing so much that I simply start to dance, right in the middle of the street. Then an American jeep catches up with us. In the front, our friend John is steering using his feet, waving like mad with his arms. The others also wave, and shout, "Russia! No more war!"

What are they saying? "Russia" — that sounds like "Russki," but what does "nou mooa wooa" mean?

We can't understand it. The Americans are besides themselves. They flap their arms around like birds flap their wings. They hug each other and clasp our hands. We can't understand what they say, but we shout with them, "Nou mooa wooa!"

The jeep turns off. We continue on our way.

Ahead of us, the town comes into view. It is quite small. We don't know what it is called. In December we hadn't even dared to lift our heads in order to read the name. Now it appears welcomingly green between low houses in the May sunshine.

"Where to now?" asks Tamara.

"No idea," I admit quite openly. "Perhaps there will be trains running from here."

"I can't imagine they would be," she answers.

"Then we'll just have to go on foot. The main thing is to get home as quickly as possible."

"You're mad! Go to Russia on foot? Do you know how many kilometers that is?"

We go straight to the station. We recognize it immediately. It is the one on whose platform we trembled with fear five months ago.

Now the station has been badly damaged, but the sign displaying its name has stayed intact. "Salzgitter" we read. I make enquiries of a German, and he tells us that no passenger trains are running yet because the railway tracks are damaged and some bridges have been blown up.

We go onto the platform. Amazing! A goods train is standing by the platform! Next to it is a struggling horde of people: Belgians and Frenchmen, Czechs and Poles. All of them are in a strange land against their will. The many different languages mingle together to make one overwhelming noise.

Nobody knows where the goods train is going. Its old, open cars are full to the brim with coal. But it's obvious that the train will be starting soon. The locomotive in front is already puffing away, and it cloaks the people running to and fro on the platform in thick black smoke clouds.

I push my way closer to the train and, in German, ask an elderly man, "Sir does this train go to Russia?"

"To Russia? My dear, no train will be going to Russia yet."

"Where is it going? We want to go home."

"You can come with us, but going home — that's not possible at the moment."

The man has answered in German, but with such a strange accent that I can't decide what nationality he is.

"Are you Russian, then?" he asks.

"That's right."

"And how old are you?"

"Sixteen."

"Sixteen? And still so small! You haven't grown much, have you."

"I grew all right until the war, but then I stopped growing," I answer sadly.

"Mm . . . you've probably come from a camp. Well, like I said, if you want to come too, climb aboard." And with one bound he leaps over the high side of the train car.

"Come on, Tamara. We'll go too," I call. "Maybe that way we'll get home more quickly. It's better to keep on the move than to wait here for ages."

We climb over the high side of the car. Someone gives us a shove from below and we roll head over heels onto the coals. When I have dusted myself down and raised my head, two young men who are already sitting there burst out laughing.

Tamara holds a piece of broken mirror in front of my face. "Look at yourself," she says.

I look at myself and also have to laugh. I look like a real Cinderella! My entire face and my blond curls are powdered with coal dust.

"Right, girls, let's introduce ourselves," says a good-looking boy with black hair and sky-blue eyes. "I am French, from Marseille. I am called Jean."

The other boy has blond hair, just like a Russian,

and good-humored gray eyes. He is called Michel and comes from Belgium.

In order to make a better impression, I introduce myself using my full name, Tatjana. The blue-eyed Jean, however, only has eyes for Tamara right from the very start.

When the train finally gets going, Jean says, "France, here we come!"

"France?" I don't understand anything anymore. "Only France? We need to get to Russia."

Michel explains, "The coal is being taken west, and we didn't want to wait until the Americans had arranged a special train for prisoners of war, so we took this one. Even if it is uncomfortable, we'll get home more quickly. It is only an open train car, mind you. If it rains, we'll get soaked through."

"So what. We're not made of sugar," says Jean, still looking at Tamara.

In the meantime it is getting dark. We have been shaken up by the day's events, and the first thing we do is sort out somewhere to sleep. Nobody has anything with them, only what we are wearing. I am only thinly clad, and of course there are no blankets. There is nothing but black coal. I look around me. Heads are popping up from other cars too, getting darker-haired by the minute. The French are going home — but I? Where am I going?

I wriggle and fidget without finding a comfortable position. Sometimes the coal sticks in my side, sometimes it sticks into my back. At last I throw aside some of the coal underneath me and make myself a cave. I crawl inside and hope that I will soon fall asleep.

A hefty jolt and the crashing of the train brakes wake me up. The train is stationary. It is already starting to get light. Far away to the horizon, as far as the eye can see, there is nothing but heaps of rubble.

"Aachen," I read. The name is scrawled in paint on the half derelict wall of the station.

Will it ever be possible to rebuild all that? I wonder. Just to clear all the piles of stone and brick will take an age. And what manpower it will need! Germany, Germany, what have you done? What a lot of suffering you have brought mankind. First you destroyed the towns of other nations, and now you lie in ruins yourself.

"Tatjana." Jean interrupts my bitter musings. "Come, Tatjana, breakfast is ready."

Rye bread, some green leaves, and radishes lie on an improvised table made of heaped-up coal. Somebody has even found some water.

Jean makes a speech. "Well my friends, today we are only drinking cold water, but I give you my word that in three or four days, if our train gets a move on, we will be in Marseille, drinking a beverage fit for the gods. That I promise you."

The May sun rises behind the horizon and sends us her first warm rays. The train drives slowly, the old cars rattle, and we sit right on top, dirty from flying ash and coal dust, but as happy as kings.

Suddenly, Jean and Michel get up and stare hard into the distance. What is there to see? I also look in that direction, but I see nothing but ruins on both sides of the track.

All at once people holding flags and banners appear along the embankment. They are shouting something.

"The border!" cheers Michel. "That is Belgium! Tatjana, Tamara! Belgium!" He is laughing and crying all at the same time.

We all hold hands and shout, "Good morning, Belgium!"

The people on the embankment, on the wide meadows, on the rooftops, are waving flags and red scarves.

"The first train! The first train out of captivity!" Michel translates the shouts of the crowd for us.

I am happy and call out joyfully with the others, but suddenly a worrying thought occurs to me. This welcome is not for me. I look at Tamara and can't recognize her. What's the matter? Her eyes are shining and she can't take her eyes off Jean.

Tamara says, "Tanja, I am going to France with Jean. I want to marry him."

"But you've only just met him! What about me? We wanted to go home and study rather than get married."

"I have changed my mind," says Tamara. "You could come with us if you wanted. Jean doesn't mind, and he would help you find Honoré."

That is a blow. Now what? France is certainly a friendly country, and perhaps we would find Honoré. But what about Mama? She would think I had died.

"Michel," I call. "Tamara is going to go to France. That's too far for me. I want to go home. What shall I do? Where should I get off?"

"We will be reaching my hometown soon, Tatjana. You could come and stay with us if you like. I have nice parents and a younger sister. They would all be happy to see you, I'm sure. And then we could make plans for the future."

This suggestion sounds sensible, and I have no alternative but to fall in with it.

My farewell to Tamara is cool. I can't easily forgive her for letting me down so quickly after all that we have been through together.

Michel says, "Pack your things, Tatjana."

There is nothing to pack. I have nothing. Michel takes me by the hand and we jump down onto the platform of the half-ruined station. Michel's eyes sparkle; his face beams. After the bitter years in a strange country and in camps, he is now back on his native soil again.

"Freedom, freedom, long-awaited freedom!" he shouts, cupping his hands like a megaphone and turning around like a spinning top.

And then, to my intense embarrassment, he puts his arms around me and hugs me tightly.

We go through the clean alleys of the small Belgian town for a quite a distance. Loud, merry music blares from the wide-open windows. Flower garlands are hung across the street from window to window, making a ceiling of flowers. They create a festive atmosphere.

Tables with brightly colored umbrellas have been put up directly on the pavement, and happy people are sitting around them, talking joyfully. Everyone is singing and rejoicing all around us. And here again there are flags and banners. One of them says, in Russian, "Thank you, Russians! A toast to your victory!"

I start to think about it. This "thank you" isn't meant for me, of course, as I haven't helped to win the victory, but I am still pleased, as a Russian.

"What are you thinking about, Tatjana?" asks Michel.

"Me? Oh, nothing. Will we get to your house soon?"

"It's right here, just around the corner." Michel is getting more and more excited.

We come to a small house with high, pointed gables and a red-tiled roof. The whole street is sparkling clean — even the pavement is so spotless and white that one could sit down and have afternoon tea on it.

Michel bursts into the house. I stay on the doorstep. An old lady is standing in the middle of the living room; she claps her hands together and throws herself into Michel's arms, crying. That must be his mother, I decide. Another, younger woman runs up and hugs him. They all huddle tightly together in the middle of the room, laughing and crying at the same time, and hugging and kissing each other.

Michel has obviously forgotten all about me. I stand by the door and feel very alone. I have the feeling that I am an unwanted extra. No one was expecting me here.

At last Michel waves in my direction and says something in a language I don't know. They all step toward me and make me welcome. The young woman kisses me and says in German, "I am Michel's sister Elizabeth, but please call me Lisa."

Everyone sits down for lunch. A large bowl filled with a greenish-yellow vegetable stands in the middle of the table. There is nothing else, but it tastes good.

"This is asparagus. We grow it ourselves," explains Lisa. "Before the war we used to eat it with butter. It tastes even better with butter."

Then it's time for coffee. Lisa groans. "This is coffee substitute. We've forgotten what real coffee smells like; it's such a long time since we had it."

After we have eaten, Michel sits down in a corner of the living room and, gesticulating wildly, tells his parents something. It must be about his experiences in Germany, I muse.

Lisa puts her arm round me and shows me the house.

In the living room stand a table and chairs. The whole of the opposite wall is obscured by plants. From here, a door leads directly out onto a courtyard. It is covered with white paving stones that shine in the sunlight. The courtyard is bordered by the walls of the neighboring houses. There is no access from the street. Boxes filled with plants hang from the walls.

"Here, this is the asparagus we ate at lunchtime," says Lisa. "We got into the habit of growing it in boxes during the war, and we harvest quite a reasonable quantity. Things went badly for us during the war, Tanja, and even now our life isn't easy. We didn't have to endure what you Russians suffered, of course.

We are a small country and didn't have the strength to resist the German invasion for very long. We also never had to cope with a famine like yours in Leningrad. No, we didn't experience that kind of suffering, and that's why we are recovering from the war more quickly. We have a roof over our heads, music, nice cafés. But we have our own problems. There is terrible unemployment. I am unemployed myself, and I can't find work anywhere. My parents weave wicker baskets. There isn't much packing material to be had at the moment, so people are buying baskets instead of boxes and suitcases. That's what we are living on. . . . Still, the war is over and that's the main thing. You must stay with us for a little while, Tanja, to recover. Come on, I'll take you upstairs and show you where you'll be sleeping."

Lisa leads me to the first floor, where there are three small bedrooms. In the bedrooms there are only wardrobes and beds made of very smooth white boards.

That evening, as I lie in one of the clean white beds I missed for so many years, I think: It's lovely here. Music, flowers, warmth — what more do I need? At home everything is in ruins, my family killed long ago — how could anyone survive such a war? I have suffered enough. Now I'm just going to enjoy myself for once, where things will go well for me.

Next morning, after breakfast, which is a slice of bread and coffee substitute, Lisa takes me to see her sister.

"Maria is very kind," says Lisa lovingly. "She is a seamstress. She often makes things for all of us. The only thing is, you always have to wait quite a long time until it's ready. Still, she'll make something for you pretty quickly. We'll ask her at once."

Just as Lisa had said, an attractive, lively woman comes to greet us. I like the look of her immediately.

"Maria," says Lisa. "Tanja is in dire need of a dress. Just look at the rags she's wearing."

"I'll gladly make something, but what from?"

The sisters think about it. Then Maria rummages in a large woven basket and pulls out a piece of faded material.

"This is curtain material," she says. "It's still good. I'll make a wonderful dress with it. I'll embroider 'Tanja' on it in blue thread. That will look lovely."

The very next day Maria brings the dress for me. "Here, Tanja, try it on!" she says.

I am thrilled with it. The dress is so lovely. The large pocket at the front is particularly smart; it has my name embroidered on it in blue silk.

I put the dress on and go over to the mirror. How many years is it since I have seen my whole reflection? Is that really me? A strange girl with light-blue eyes looks back at me. Her face is a little pale, but golden curls fall around it. Is that me? Yes, that's you, that's you, I assure myself happily. Perhaps I could even be described as quite pretty?

"And Cinderella turned into a beautiful princess!" says Michel, stepping beside the mirror.

All at once they all begin to discuss my future. Michel says, "I would like Tanja to stay with us forever."

Lisa says that that is what she also wants, because she has come to love me like a sister. Maria promises me that she'll sort out my clothes, and she says that they will need to look after me for quite some time until I have recovered completely and am able to look after myself.

But now, Joseph, Maria's husband, who has been quiet for some time, speaks. "Tanja is a bright girl and still very young. It's imperative for her to learn something. People without a good education are already finding it hard to get work, and it will get even harder in the future. But it will be difficult for her to get a good education and business training here, in our little Belgium. In fact, being away from one's own homeland is no joke. Tanja might well be very happy at first, but later she will feel homesick."

"The war has stolen her childhood and youth," retorts Lisa. "She has endured a great deal and suffered much. Now at least let her live a little."

But I have understood. Even though Lisa wishes me nothing but good with all her heart, Joseph is right, not she.

After this minor disagreement we all go for a walk in the town park in order to have our photograph taken. Maria and Michel both want to stand next to me. I don't want to hurt anybody. They are all so kind to me: Maria, Lisa, Michel, Joseph. But whichever way we position ourselves in front of the camera, someone is always standing too far away from me. Then I have an idea. "You all stay standing. I'll lie in the grass, at your feet," I say, and I lie stretched out to my full length.

Joseph laughs. "There, you see, now everyone has their share of Tanja."

July 1945. The days go by and I live here as carefree as I was in my childhood. The summer of 1945 is wonderful in Belgium: sun, music, flowers, and more flowers. The people are celebrating their freedom, and the celebration shows no sign of coming to an end. It is so easy and relaxing to live one day at a time. I try not to think of my home: I am so afraid that Mama will no longer be there.

One morning Lisa says, "Tanja, today we are going to a wealthy family that gives to charity."

"What does that mean, charity?"

"That means that the rich help the poor," she explains.

"And how do they help? Do they share out their wealth?" I ask, disbelievingly.

"No, not exactly." Lisa hesitates. "They give things to the poor. Clothes and food, for example."

On our way, Lisa says, "It would be nice if they could give you something warm for the winter. Yes, that's what I'll ask for. Even though winter isn't all that cold here, you don't have anything warm to wear."

We come to a formal entrance. A footman opens the door. Lisa explains something to him in Flemish, at length. At last he allows us into the house. The housekeeper comes. She listens to Lisa and leads us into the next room. She goes away and leaves us standing there.

This must be where we will be seen. A few chairs covered in light-colored velvet stand against the walls. I sit down carefully on the edge of one of the chairs. Lisa doesn't sit down. She gives me the impression that she is very nervous.

"Come on, Lisa, let's go home," I suggest. "I feel stupid, waiting here for charity."

"Soon. In a moment," she replies.

At last a tall, fashionable lady comes in. She looks at us sternly, and in a not very friendly way. Lisa again explains something for a long time. The lady goes. Again we wait for a long time. At last she appears with a small bag. She says something briefly and nods her head at the same time. Then she goes. Lisa smiles and curtseys. I find the whole thing mortifying. She did all that for my sake. Why did I let myself be persuaded into it? The war is over. We are all at liberty. Why must we beg for alms?

Lisa is also disappointed. The bag contains a few cotton shirts. She had been hoping for some warm clothes.

"I don't need anything," I tell her. "I don't want charity. It offends me. You can throw that stuff away. I won't wear it."

"But you have accepted things from us!" replies Lisa, astonished.

"Yes, from you — that is different. You would give away the last thing you possessed, and give it from the heart. But this is like giving alms to a beggar, and I am not a beggar, nor a prisoner any more, either. In fact, more than anything I want to work for my keep. I have rested enough."

Next day I say to Lisa, "Let's try and find work."

"We could do that," answers Lisa flatly. She doesn't seem very enthusiastic about my decision, but I hope that she understands my reasons.

At the first business where we ask for work, the people are very welcoming. A pleasant man in a gray suit looks at me with interest and smiles in a friendly way while Lisa hastily explains something in Flemish. As I already know one or two Flemish words, I guess that they are talking about my experiences as a prisoner of war in Germany and the things I endured there.

When Lisa finishes, he starts to speak. Lisa's face clouds over. She interrupts him, but the man shakes his head. It is clear to me what that means.

"Let's go," said Lisa. "There's no work here."

"Not for you either?" I ask.

"Not for me either."

That day we traipse around many factories and assorted businesses, going up and down stairs on spiral staircases, marble steps, squeaky and luxurious stairs, up and down, up and down.

At the end of the day I am completely exhausted. We have been turned down everywhere.

Despite this we want to try again the next day.

"Today we'll go to a large factory," says Lisa. "It's quite a way away from us. Actually I'd rather you didn't work there; it's heavy industry. But perhaps it also involves some lighter work."

We set off. Practically everyone goes on foot or by bicycle in this small town. At first the path leads through wasteland, then it goes past dumps and factory houses.

At last we come to a huge building. It looks quite sinister. My heart contracts. I remember a similar factory in Germany and my sleepless nights there. But I erase the bitter memories from my mind. Now everything is different. There is no such thing as forced labor any more.

We are shown to the entrance and go timidly into a large office. A fat man sits at his desk.

"No," he says, after he has listened to what Lisa has to say. He turns to speak to me, and adds in German, "I have no work for you. You are much too weak for our business. But if you would like to work as a nurse or housemaid, I could find you a private position quite easily."

"No," I say, equally firmly. "I must learn, and for that I need work of a different kind."

The man is outraged. "We have unemployment, and yet you quibble about the kind of work you want? We have absolutely no work here. Your companion" — he indicates Lisa — "is out of work herself, and I have nothing to offer her. We don't even have work for our own people, and you are a foreigner. No, I can't help you." He stands up and indicates that the interview is over.

On the way home we are both unhappy. Lisa stays silent, crushed. I begin to ponder my situation. They don't have any work for their own people, and I don't even belong here. Of course, Lisa and Michel are kind people. They are sympathetic and want to help me. But I can't let myself be mothered by them forever. I have to look after myself. The best I can hope for here is unskilled labor, and I wouldn't even be able to hold on to my dream of studying.

What will become of me? Am I really going to stay uneducated all my life? No! Back at home in Russia, everyone must be needed. There is such a lot to do there, and they will almost certainly want to encourage education. That would mean I could study and put down roots, even if Mama is not there anymore.

When we get home and into the living room, I say, "Lisa, I have been thinking seriously about things. I want to go home. I like being with you, but no one needs me here. I can't even find work, and I so want to achieve something. You know, there is a Russian proverb: 'Where you were born, that's where you are needed.'"

At this point Michel comes into the house. He goes

to a special labor exchange every day, where he is given compensation for his war injuries and they try to find work for him. When Lisa tells him of my decision, Michel looks sad. "Stay in Belgium, Tanja," he says. "We will be able to cope with any problems together."

"No, Michel. I was born in Russia and I want to return to my country, to my native soil."

"Your country is in ruins, and your native soil has been devastated."

"Exactly. That's another reason why I must go home."

"You are choosing a difficult path. Will you have enough strength to go through with it?"

"I must try, whatever."

However confused my feeling are, I have made my decision. Now it is time to do something about it.

I turn to Lisa. "Will you go with me to Brussels, Lisa? Please help me to find my embassy. I really must go home now."

Two weeks later I am traveling east on a train.

August 1945. Huge American Studebakers speed past on the wide motorways. The bright August sun burns down on the streets and makes the air shimmer. The ruins of German towns and sleepy villages are left far behind. My heart beats faster with impatience. At last we reach the Elbe and the town of Torgau. It is here that the American army and our soldiers met.

Now, at last, I will soon be seeing my own people, people from my homeland. The bridge over the Elbe is within sight already, and the striped American flag is fluttering there. The guards on the bridge salute. "Farewell, farewell," I call to the smiling young men. I must go farther on, to the other side, the Russian side.

We pick our way across the damaged bridge. I can already see the red flags. We all shout, "Hurray!" Soldiers with red armbands salute and wave to us. "Oh you heroes! How I love you," I whisper, and I stretch my hands out toward them as far as I can, until I nearly fall out of the truck. How wonderful to have survived. What happiness it is to be alive!

The Studebakers turn and drive back to the American zone. We — that is, all those returning from captivity — are given shelter in some apartments in Torgau. In a few days we will be going home and the first military trains will be returning to our country. I run around, singing loudly, and can't even recognize my own voice. Only a few months ago we were unhappy, bitter people. But now we are laughing and dancing again.

Within a few days I have made friends with the

people living with me in the apartments. Today, when we woke up, we had a pillow fight. Down and feathers flew out of the pillows and billowed around the room. We are nearly mad with joy! Today we will be going home at last.

Three of us stand with our bundles on the station platform, warming ourselves in the sunshine and waiting for the command to get on board. The military train has been standing ready for some time, but the order has still not been given.

We hear, "Get aboard. Women with children and old people first!"

The carriages fill up quickly. And what about us? We are told, "You must wait!"

We don't know what to do. Then we hear that there aren't enough locomotives and carriages. We will have to stay in Torgau a little longer.

Summer 1946. I have lived in Torgau for nearly a year, waiting for the trains to sort themselves out and earning a little money by doing odd jobs here and there. I am feeling much stronger now, but my happy life here is clouded by two things. Firstly, I seem to be constantly hungry, even though I am very well provided for. I eat three courses, but I have hardly eaten them before I could eat all over again. Will his hunger never leave me? That would be awful!

The second worry troubles me much more. I have allowed myself to start hoping that perhaps Mama has survived the war. But if she has survived it, where is she? And what about Aunt Anja and Aunt Kapa, who stayed in Leningrad? I know what a dreadful siege the city had to endure. I fear I must be the only one left. I was only rescued by a miracle myself, after all.

My friends try to cheer me up. "Don't give up, write. The post office is back in order again at last. They will be able to find your relatives. Someone will be sure to give you some news."

But to whom shall I write? At what address? I remember that Aunt Anja lived by the canal in Leningrad. But the house? The apartment number? No, I can't remember it. I write the address like this: To Solonizyna Anna Fjodorowna, The Canal, Leningrad.

A month later I receive a reply from Leningrad — from Aunt Anja. "Your mama is alive, and Aunt Tassja. I survived the siege, but Aunt Kapa and her little daughter Adotschka died in the artillery fire. All the men in our family were killed. How did you manage to stay alive, Tanja? Your mama has long since given up hope and thinks of you as dead and buried. She has wept for you as if you had been killed. Your mama is not very well, nor is your sister. But we are all very happy that you have miraculously reappeared, and we are waiting for you at home. Come soon. You didn't put the right address, but the postman found the house, even so."

Autumn 1946. The train brings me back home to Russia at last. I am glad that my love of life has not left me. It won't be driven out, neither by captivity nor forced labor. I am full of hope in rainbow colors — and my dearest wish is to learn.

The train brings me nearer and nearer home. We pass the Russian border. This is where my homeland begins!

My thoughts go round in time to the music of the wheels. Where shall I begin? I am uneducated. And what if I want to study? Do I have enough strength and willpower for that?

The train hurries toward Leningrad. Just a few more minutes and we will arrive at the station. All at once the train stops. It is waiting for a light to turn green. But I can't bear to wait anymore. Shall I jump out and run?

At last we start to move forward; slowly, much too slowly! There is the platform. I jump out. The earth under my feet feels as light as feathers. I am floating on air.

Here is the canal. There is Aunt Anja's house. I dash up to the fourth floor like lightning.

"Aunt Anja! It's me!"

Aunt Anja used to be beautiful. In fact, all my mother's sisters were beautiful: tall northerners, blond with blue eyes. Now the sparkle in Aunt Anja's eyes has been extinguished. She stands there diminished, half-starved.

"How wonderful that you are here again, Tanja! You must live with me for a while. The Platonows' house in Wyritza where you lived during the war was burned down by the SS as they retreated," she explains. "Your mama lives sometimes in one place, then another. I help her as much as I can."

That same day I hurry onward, to Mama in Wyritza.

Mama is unrecognizable. When we said good-bye she was still young. Marked by hunger, but still young. Now an old lady is standing in front of me. Outside it is autumn, but she is barefoot. She has no shoes.

My sister Olja also looks terrible: large eyes, long legs, but thin — just skin and bone. One ear is bandaged. Discharge is oozing from it.

"It was dreadful," says Mama. "Olja nearly froze during the war, Tanja. Then her legs just wouldn't work any more. I had to carry her on my back throughout the whole of the war."

"I know, Mama, I can see. We mustn't lose any more time. First we'll go and buy you shoes. Winter is coming soon. I earned a little money in Torgau. That will last us for a while. I will try to find a warm room for you, and then I will start studying. I have worked it all out."

"How do you think you will manage it, Tanja?" says Mama doubtfully. "You are nearly eighteen now and your education stopped at thirteen. Don't you think you should start working straight away? I can't help you anymore."

Mother must have suffered terrible things, to go against her own beliefs. Before the war she always said, "Education is the most important thing." And now she no longer believes in her own words. And what has happened to her musical voice? And her eyes don't shine any more. It's as if she is no longer the person she once was. Mama, Mama, what has the war done to you?

I try to calm her as best I can. "Don't worry, Mama. We'll think of something. We'll put Olja back on her feet, too. But I must learn, at all costs. I'll do it quickly, you'll see!"

"Well, I don't know." She shakes her head disbelievingly.

"Don't be afraid, Mama, I'll manage."

Unfortunately it turns out that there is no school for young, working people in Wyritza, and the children's school which they have just set up won't take me. They say I am already too old.

So I go back the sixty kilometers to Leningrad, to stay with Aunt Anja. "You can study in Leningrad and live with me," she says.

The school for young people is not far from Aunt Anja's house. I go there that very same day.

"I want to study."

"Of course," says the school director. "You just have to give me an enrollment certificate."

I go the military office.

"Please give me a certificate. I so long to go to school again."

The head of the military area, red-cheeked and scrubbed clean, doesn't understand. "What's all this about? Show me your passport."

"My passport? I don't have a passport. I wasn't old enough to have my own before the war."

"Then you can't get a certificate. You have to have a passport to get a certificate."

"What shall I do, then?"

"I don't know. You could try another town."

"What do you mean — another town? I don't know anyone in another town. I was born here. My aunt lives here and I can stay with her."

"That doesn't interest me," he replies curtly, looking at me with cold eyes.

His gaze makes me feel uneasy. I suddenly have a terrifying thought: "No one has been waiting for you here, either, in your own homeland. You are not even wanted here."

I say, almost pleadingly, "But I have endured a great deal."

"Others have too, and you're too old for school, anyway. It's time for you to get married."

"Not for a long time," I tell him, without any pleading tone now. "It is never too late to learn. I don't believe you. I believe in the power of the Soviet Union, and now I shall go and find it."

"You can look for it, but not here." He gives me back my application form. It is marked, "Refused."

That can't be true! I think, as I find myself outside the door. Has everyone forgotten the way things were before the war? Even Mama has said that the war has driven out all her memories. However, there is no sense in complaining. I must fight for what I want.

That night there are heavy knocks on the door. It's the military. Aunt Anja is frightened. She says, "This is my niece. She is visiting me."

"She has twenty-four hours to pack her bags," explains the military officer. "That is the rule."

I start to weep. "What shall I do, Aunt Anja?" But she doesn't know.

The next night the military officer comes again.

"You're still here? Make sure that you have disappeared before tomorrow morning, otherwise I'll place you under arrest."

What shall I do? I can't understand all this. Even when I was a prisoner in a terrible fascist regime, I still found good people. Are there none in Russia? That can't be.

"Aunt Anja, who is the boss, the highest official in the military?"

"The military commander in Leningrad is General Solowjow. His office is in Palace Square. You must apply to him."

I write my application to Solowjow himself. "I completed five years at school before the war. I was an excellent pupil. I dreamed about becoming an actress, but the war destroyed all my dreams. Now I have come back to my homeland and I so want to continue my education. Please help me. I give you my word that I will not disappoint you and that I will become a worthwhile person."

Aunt Anja reads the application and says, "That's not how you fill in an application. You haven't even used the form."

I send it off anyway. I have only written what I believe, and I can vouch for every word.

I am given a date for an interview. It is on December 31, the last day of the year. Until then I cannot study or go to work. No one will take me. But I have a lot to do. I go to the Bronnitzki Hospital with my sister in order to have her ears looked at.

The doctors are horrified. "Why have you let this go on so long? Such a pretty girl, and now she will always be deaf."

"We couldn't come earlier," I say, very upset. "The war."

December 17, 1946. There are still two weeks until my interview. All my hopes rest on this date. Meanwhile I am staying with friends of Aunt Anja. I can't stay with her. The military come every night and ask where I am. Aunt Anja explains that I have gone away to another town and she doesn't know the name of it.

I can't stay with Mama. I haven't been able to find her a room. She is living in a tiny hut in Wyritza. It's good that no snow has fallen yet.

I go to see her. When I look at her, worn-out with grief, and my invalid sister, frustration grips me. But at least Mama is slowly regaining a little strength.

"They have set up the Invalids' Working Group again," she tells me. "I am working in the pottery. Once I have earned something, then perhaps I can rent a room and buy bread for my supper."

Mama and I sit in the cold hut and drink hot tea.

Olja is lying on a heap of rags. The rags have been thrown on top of a homemade structure that serves as a bed. Olja can hardly walk. She has weak legs, and her ears are bound up.

"Well," says Mama. "You can forget white sheets and starched bedcovers. The word 'hygiene' has long been out of use here."

"Tell me, Mama, what happened to you in the war?"

"Oh, don't ask. That's something I can't bear to go through again, even in my imagination." Even so, she begins hesitantly. "After they had taken you young people off to Germany, they soon started to take the rest of us, too. The Nazi soldiers came to the houses with trucks and horse-drawn carts, and put us on them along with our children and everything we had."

"And you didn't protest?"

"What are you talking about! All this was happening at the point of a machine gun! The day before, I had gone to see a neighbor for some reason or other. It was strangely quiet in her house. I looked in her room: She was lying there, bloated. I looked more closely: She was dead. Her little son was sitting on the floor, playing. I was nearly fainting with hunger myself, but I picked the little one up. After that I had two to look after. They put the three of us onto the horse-drawn cart in the frost and the rain, and they took us away to a district that we didn't know. My sister Tassja and I were separated. She went to Estland, I went to Lithuania. We were unloaded in a village."

"But what did they want with you? You were ill and starving!"

"I don't understand that myself. They said that they were collecting us for a possible later swap with prisoners of war. They didn't believe then that they would lose the war."

"And in Lithuania, what happened to you there?"

"The Lithuanian women took pity on us and the children. They turned an old bathing hut into a home for us, and every morning they put a jug of milk and a piece of bread on the windowsill. They called me the 'city lady,' even though I was dressed in rags. Perhaps it was became I was the only one in the village who was able to read and write.

"The floor in our hut was made of clay. That's why Olja caught a chill in the winter. The boy stayed healthy, though. As soon as our own army came to Lithuania, I set off for home. People wanted to talk me out of it. They said it was a long, hard road. But I still went. For a whole month I made my way through to Wyritza with the children; on foot, on horseback, and in a cart. How we escaped death, God alone knows. . . .

"I made it to Wyritza. Everything had been turned to rubble and ashes. Not a house was left standing. But at least I had kept my passport safe. Before they came to take us away I had put it into a box and buried it in the woods. It's a good thing I remembered that. People who didn't have a passport had great problems when they tried to register as survivors later."

"And what did you do with the little boy?"

"After we returned to Wyritza I had to put him in a children's home. I couldn't look after two. I had enough trouble staying on my own feet."

"The things you endured, Mama."

December 27, 1946. It is very cold. I must find Mama a room. Mama and I go through Wyritza, searching. So many people have been made homeless, it is very hard to find somewhere for a reasonable rent. We step out onto the Siwersker highway. The Siwersker highway! I saw so much human suffering here.

Mama has little hope that we will find a warm room. "During the war, many houses were destroyed by bombs. The others were set alight by the Germans as they retreated. The Soviet leaders in the village won't allow any building. They say that there aren't any building materials."

All at once we are standing in front of a heap of rubble. I can hardly recognize this once familiar spot.

"This was where the Platonows' house used to stand! The one we lived in at the beginning of the war!"

"Yes," says Mama. "This was their property. But there is no sign of the Platonows themselves. They didn't come back after the war."

We have good luck and find a room in a large house. I help bring Mama's things over. Now all we have to do is to look around for firewood.

The last few days before my interview at the Palace Square drag unbearably. At last it is time. It is December 31. The last day before the year 1947. Early in the morning I make my way to the Palace Square. I go into the large waiting room. Chairs stand around the walls, and there are people sitting on all of them. They look sad. Everyone here has worries, it seems.

We are seen in order. When people disappear behind the massive door, they seem very nervous. Then it is my turn. I have butterflies. The door seems to be very heavy. It just won't budge. I pull and pull — before I notice that I just have to push it.

I enter the room. I see a large desk, and a gray-haired general sitting behind it. But the office doesn't look the way you would expect a general's office to look. It is small and modest.

The general reads my application. Then he raises his head and says, "What's wrong, Tanjuscha. Have you come back home to a grudging welcome?"

This time tears squeeze out of their own accord. I sob, "I haven't been welcomed at all, Sir General."

"Well now, girl, don't cry. Everything will work out for the best. We have suffered enough. Now we will start from the beginning again, learning how to live happy lives."

His kind words make my tears flow even more.

I have hardly calmed down before I ask a question that has been tormenting me for some time. "I would so like to study, but the country has been completely destroyed. Should I not try to help rebuild it, and go to work?"

"Listen, Tanja. I think you should most certainly start by studying. We can build without you, Tan-juscha. But we have not only lost the talents of practical men, we have also lost educated ones. We will need doctors and engineers and scientists. Have you already thought about what you would like to be?"

"Of course, I've thought about it a great deal."

"If I remember rightly, there is no one to support you at the moment. You don't have a father anymore, and your mother, you say, is ill."

"That's true, but I can look after myself. I have decided to become a teacher. I would like to teach in order to help the whole country to learn reading and writing more quickly, so that everyone can have a better grasp of history."

"That's good. Teachers are also needed desperately." The general hands me a document. "Everything will improve now, Tanjuscha."

Beside myself with joy I hurry out into the Palace Square, toward the main street, Newski-Prospekt. I must get on the tram quickly! No, not the tram. It takes too long. It'll be quicker on foot. I fly across the Newski-Prospekt, start to skip, and say to myself, "I am the luckiest person in the world, the very luckiest. I will be able to study!" I must say that quite loud, because people turn around and look at me. They look at me, and smile.

January 1947. Today I have begun to keep a real diary again. It is an unbelievably long time since I first wrote in it. Then it was before the war, when I was having so many happy days that I wanted to find some way to remember them. After that, when the troubles started, I wrote my diary in my imagination. But now it is January 1947 and we have survived the worst.

At last I have got a passport and registration card from the military, but before they would give it to me they questioned me for a whole day. They kept asking who I am, why I was taken by the Germans, why I only came back after a year, and thousands of other questions. They filled up a whole stack of forms. I said to the man who was questioning me, "Here is the commander's warrant that I can register as a local citizen. Why do we have to waste so much time for nothing? We have lost enough time because of the war."

But he said, "Why should I be interested in what the commander has to say? We have to be extremely careful. Someone who has been abroad could have come back as a spy."

Even when I left the military office, holding my passport in my hands, I was still very frightened. Perhaps they would call me back? They don't trust me. But why? Just because I was taken abroad?

January 12, 1947. Oh, I'm so happy! At last I can go to school again. I get to school and the director asks me, "Do you have your report book with you?"

"The report book? No, that was lost in the war."

"You wanted to join . . . Year Eight, is that right? Which year were you when the war began?"

I looked down at my feet and mumbled, "Year Seven." It was Year Five, really, but he doesn't need to know that.

"How on earth did you manage that!" He obviously doesn't believe me. "So you want to go straight into Year Eight?" he repeated. He looked at me sternly. "You've missed half the school year already. How will you catch up?"

"I will work day and night. I'm sure I'll catch up."

"Good. Then I'll put you into Year Eight, and we'll see how you get on."

The same evening I go along for the first time. I arrive an hour before the start of the lesson. As I enter the classroom, my heart beats wildly. No one else is there yet.

I sit down in one of the rows and look at the old school bench. It was black once, but now it has been scribbled so full of letters, signs, pluses and minuses, that it's taken on a gray-brown color. But it means a great deal to me. I smooth my hand over the bench, lay my head on the old desk lid, and press my cheek against it, thinking, "My dream has come true."

January 20, 1947. Today I have admitted it to myself: I am the worst pupil in the class. I find it difficult to concentrate. Even the way I read aloud is wooden and stilted.

As for math, the less said about that the better! That dreadful algebra! It's good that Jura has sat down next to me. He is seventeen, not very tall, and still has a very childish face. He can work out sums very easily, and he helps me with them.

February 24, 1947. I have just got back from Wyritza. I go there every Saturday after my lessons to see Mama, and on Sundays I return to the town. This time I had a slight argument with Mama — the first time that we have ever disagreed.

I had hardly stepped inside the house before Mama said, "Maria Ganizina was here. She asked for you. She was looking rather depressed. She was also taken away to Germany, wasn't she? Why don't you go and visit her and find out her news?"

I remembered that before the war we had always fetched our milk from the Ganizins. Maria had already been in Year Ten, while I was only in Year Five.

When I arrived at the Ganizins, Maria was sitting on the front steps, staring sadly at nothing. By contrast, I was fizzing with joy inside. The feeling of freedom which had gripped me at the end of the war had not really left me yet. The hurdles that I had first encountered and which had threatened to overturn all my dreams had been quickly mastered, and I felt as if nothing could ever silence my inner rejoicing. Maria had also survived. Why was she so sad?

"Have you been back long?" she asked in a tired voice.

"Yes, quite a while. I am going to school now, so I am very happy," I burst out. But I noticed immediately that my loud, happy voice stood in stark contrast to Maria's sorrow.

"It's good that you have managed to do that. You were lucky. But most of us who were taken to Germany as captive workers were taken away again after we had returned home. We weren't even allowed to say good-bye to our relatives. But this time we were transported to a Soviet camp, for tree-felling. Even prisoners of war had to go there, and they had already suffered enough torment in German captivity. Do you know what they call us now? 'Traitors.' Can you imagine that? 'Traitors!'"

Shaking her head, Maria stood up and went into the house.

"The poor thing," said Mama, when I had told her Maria's story. "But it's true that we need firewood for the nurseries and the hospitals. Who else could have provided that after the war? The wounded who had returned home? The women who had survived the siege? That is what the terrible war has done to people."

"How can you say that?" I retorted. "If they had said to Maria, 'Welcome home. We are glad that you are back, and we ask that you help the children and the wounded,' that would have been different. But instead of that she was accused of being a traitor! Is it our fault that we were taken away? Just think how they led the wounded soldiers along the Siwersker highway into German capitivity. At the time you said, 'Those poor boys . . .' You said 'poor' not 'treacherous.' In Belgium they welcomed the returning prisoners of war with flowers."

"Our people welcomed the heroic soldiers who freed us with flowers," Mama replied. "Belgium surrendered early on. Just imagine what would have happened if we had not endured. We have freed ourselves from fascism; you are going to school. What more do you want?"

"Of course I am grateful to those who freed us," I answered. "But you, Mama, you always taught me to listen to my conscience and to help those in trouble. Shouldn't that count for the whole of our country? The country that we call the most just in the world? Can you tell me why our own countrymen, who were taken to Germany as laborers or prisoners of war, should be cursed as traitors?"

"Psst!" Mama laid a finger on her mouth. She had been making signs at me to be quiet for a while now, but I was in full flow and couldn't stop myself.

"You see," I continued. "We are all alone in an

empty house, but you are even frightened of the walls hearing! Was it really like this before the war? Those of us who longed to come home to our native land would so love to be of use. I have come home and want to build a life worth living along with everyone else. Why do people distrust me and call Maria a traitor? Are we strangers? Strangers in our own country? How can we all live together without trusting one another?"

"Oh Tanja, what are you saying?" sighed Mama. "All mothers, who would have given everything to save their children, only want peace, a roof over their heads, and maybe, like me, dream of a bread roll with their tea."

Poor Mama! When I heard her speak so unhappily and fatalistically, my heart contracted.

February 26, 1947. February is nearly over. Soon it will be spring, my favorite time of year. All week I have been sitting in front of my school books. The difficult problems are beginning to become clearer, but I sometimes stumble over the easy ones.

Today I was so absentminded because of all the things I was reading that I heated up the soup that Aunt Anja had been simmering for two days and poured it down the sink, quite automatically. The only things that remained in the saucepan were the bones. I must have had the crazy idea that I was pouring water off the boiled potatoes.

Our life is hard. We survive mainly on potatoes and vegetable stew. There are some groceries available in the shops, but Aunt Anja doesn't have much money — she helps support Mama and Aunt Tassja, as well.

June 1947. I have finished Year Eight and I am being allowed to skip Year Nine as long as I do the work independently during the summer holidays — and as long as I pass the exams.

The woman from whom Mama is renting her room has let me use her little shed to work in. The roof isn't quite watertight, but I have fixed it temporarily. The room has become a little hideaway. Nobody disturbs me here, even if I work twelve hours a day. I have drawn up a timetable and I am determined to keep to it. After all, I have to get through the whole of the Year Nine syllabus in one summer. I must work hard. Time won't wait, and Mama is in a bad way. She works very hard, but she can't afford to feed Olja without some help.

September 1947. The summer is over. At the beginning of the month Mama came to see me in my shed.

She just shook her head. "It's against all common sense. . . ."

But I did it! I have passed all my Year Nine written exams with distinction. It was a hard summer, without much time for enjoyment, but it means I am now in Year Ten.

March 1948. It's spring again already! The sun is shining more strongly now, but the snow hasn't melted yet. I haven't entered anything in my diary all winter. The work for Year Ten is terribly hard. My poor head; every day I stuff it full of such a mass of rules, dates, and theorems that it feels as if it will burst. I can't go on like this any more. I must have a break.

Today I asked my neighbor to lend me her old pair of skates. I went into the park, where the lake is still frozen. I tied the skates to my boots with a piece of cord and gingerly went out onto the ice. I was quite good at skating as a child. I glided along carefully. A young man stopped next to me and suggested that we should skate together.

"I'm not very good at skating. It's not worth it."

"That doesn't matter," he said. "I'll teach you."

We took each other by the hand and skated together. We went home together, too. He said it was on his way. He is called Sergei.

By the gate to the courtyard he said, "I like you. Shall I come back to see you tomorrow? Then we could go to the cinema."

"I can't, I'm afraid," I answered. "I have so much to do, I can't afford to let myself be distracted. There are so many gaps in my education, and I must finish school as quickly as I can. Then I'll go to the teacher training college. Don't be angry with me. . . . Goodbye!" And I ran off through the gateway.

I turned around at the corner. Sergei was still standing there, a large young man with blond hair. I like him a lot. I wanted to turn back and say, "I've changed my mind. I accept." But I fought back my secret wish.

July 1948. It's already two weeks since I passed all the exams, but I still can't quite believe it. I still don't have time for my diary. I have to study for yet more exams: the entrance exams for the teacher training college. Soon I will be a college student!

September 1949. The year since my last diary entry has gone by like lightning. It has been a hard but very happy year. Every morning when I get to the Institute and read the inscription, "Teacher Training College, Leningrad," I can hardly believe that I am studying here.

The war has been over for four years, but I am still often so hungry that my head spins while I am listening to the lectures. But now I have something that means as much to me as food: After the lectures I can sit in the library until far into the night and read books about Russian history and our great literary classics.

Sometimes I find a book that no one has opened before me. Sometimes a book has been read so many times that the print is beginning to fade. And all the thoughts, ideas, and new theories . . .

Perhaps I am just following a path that all mankind follows: a path from ignorance to understanding, from incomprehension to insight. Sometimes my head is so full to overflowing that I don't know how I will ever be able to digest the amazing amount of knowledge with which I am bombarded. What a pleasure it is to share in the accumulated wisdom that mankind has acquired. You needn't feel alone any longer. Another world is created within you, and with it an inner freedom. I need this a great deal now, when there is so little freedom in the world outside.

March 1953. I have not written in my diary for far too long. I only found the diary at all after a good deal of searching.

Stalin is dead! Our college is in official mourning. Many students and lecturers went to Moscow for the funeral. They say that people trampled each other just to get closer to the coffin. But Aunt Anja whispered today, "It could well be that people aren't crying because they mourn Stalin but because they have lost husbands and sons in the war, because they can't forget the days of the terrible siege, and because even after the war is over, their life is still so hard."

It's true that the music they are playing on the radio is so sad that it makes you start crying for no reason at all.

I don't share in the state mourning. My idol, Stalin, fell on the day that I learned from Maria Ganizina that she and others returning from captivity were being condemned as traitors.

The newspapers say that we are doing better than other countries and that the West is suffering. But I know — I saw with my own eyes — that that is not true. Even battered and in ruins, Western Europe is obviously far ahead of us. But that doesn't bother me. A high standard of living is something that is agreeable and comforting, but it is not the sum total of happiness. What I cannot bear is that we are being told lies.

I used to think that our hardship and suffering was the fault of the war. But it is not just the war. It is also lies and intimidation by the State. I would so like to thank the Americans who first came into the village and gave me, a starving girl, something to eat. And also the Germans who helped me in captivity. But I do not dare. I am even too scared to trace Honoré, to write and tell him that I still think of him. If the State were to find out, I would be called a "cosmopolitan" or "spy," and I would be hounded out of the training college — or worse. And because of this many people will think me ungrateful.

Today I have been along a much loved path for the last time. It is the path I always used throughout my student years — over the Palace Bridge, and along the Newa riverbank.

I have said good-bye to all the places that mean so much to me, for tomorrow I am traveling to a village far in the North. Soon I will be sharing all the things that I know and all my thoughts with my very first pupils.

Because as of today, I have become a teacher.

HISTORICAL NOTE

In the 1930s, fascism began to make its mark in Europe. A charismatic leader, Adolf Hitler, rose to power in Germany. Hitler persuaded his people that fascism would make Germany a great power again, and he believed that the Aryan race (his word for "racially pure" Germans) was meant to rule over the "*untermensch*," other races which he considered inferior. This appalling prejudice of Hitler's was to cost millions of people their lives.

In 1938 Hitler and Joseph Stalin, the Communist dictator of Soviet Russia, signed a nonaggression pact. In September 1939, Hitler began his campaign of conquest by invading Poland, and Stalin took the opportunity to invade Poland from the east. Poland was then divided between these two partners. In the meantime Great Britain, the British Commonwealth, and France declared war on Germany. (The United States entered the war in December 1941, when the Japanese bombed Pearl Harbor.)

On June 22, 1941, Hitler broke the nonaggression pact and launched a surprise attack, code-named Operation Barbarossa, on his former ally. The Soviets were completely unprepared, and the German army advanced at the extraordinary rate of more than fifty miles a day. Russian troops (known as the Red Army) retreated, laying waste to the land they crossed to ensure that the invaders would not benefit from local food and resources. This became known as the "scorched earth" policy. But while devastating the surrounding countryside did slow down the German advance, it also caused a terrible famine for the local people.

Hitler's first target in Russia was Moscow, but a determined Soviet counteroffensive drove his troops back. Then, in July 1942, he attacked Stalingrad. The battle was terrible. Over a million people died.

The victory at Stalingrad was a huge boost to Russian morale, and though the Germans launched an offensive in the summer of 1943, the Red Army was able to defeat them again in the greatest tank battle of all time. By the end of only one day each side had lost about 10,000 men. Hitler had had enough and called off the offensive within the week.

While Nazi Germany's young men were fighting abroad, German farms and factories experienced severe labor shortages. The Nazis decided to use the civilians of occupied countries as their labor force. By 1944 over seven million foreign men and women like Tatjana had been brought to Germany from the occupied nations.

Some laborers, particularly girls, worked in domestic service and lived with their employers, but the majority lived in the forbidding barrack blocks of labor camps. Tatjana experienced both. The workers had little direct contact with civilians other than their employers. German citizens were not allowed to mix with the enemy, and the penalty for "fraternization" could be internment in a concentration camp or even death. Both Tatjana and the Meiers risked terrible punishment when the Meiers gave her food.

The final blow for Hitler's dreams of a conquered Soviet Union came in January 1944 with the relief of Leningrad (now St. Petersburg), Tatjana's hometown. Besieged for nearly three years, more than one and a half million people died. The suffering was immense, and Russia's anger was terrible.

By the end of January 1945, the great Russian general Marshal Zhukov and his First Belorussian Front had reached the Oder river, only sixty-five kilometers to the east of Berlin. The Russian offensive on

Berlin started on April 16, 1945, preceded by intense artillery fire and blanket bombing of the surrounding area. The struggle for Berlin was one of the bloodiest battles fought this century.

On April 24, 1945, officers of the U.S. Fifth Army Corps met Russian officers on the Elbe. On April 30, Hitler committed suicide in his bunker. Berlin finally fell to the Russians on May 2, and the German *Reich* began to surrender piecemeal. Finally, a formal surrender was agreed at Allied Supreme Headquarters at two o'clock on May 7. This was confirmed at Marshal Zhukov's headquarters in Berlin on May 8.

Soviet Russia suffered terrible losses in the Second World War. An estimated ninety percent of the Allied casualties were Russian. The total number of Soviet dead came to a staggering figure of twenty million — of which seven million were soldiers and the rest were civilians. Added to this, twenty-five million people were homeless, and all were hungry. Nevertheless, people felt a great pride in their country's achievement and the USSR's new world power status. They looked forward to a better life.

But the high hopes of returning Russian prisoners were not realized. The prisoners of war and captive laborers returning from Germany were treated as traitors and spies, supposedly tainted by their stay in the capitalist West. The compulsory registration of all survivors was also very hard for those like Tatjana who did not have a passport or papers. Those who did not register often ended up in Russian labor camps. For people who had already suffered in Germany, it was a bitterly hard homecoming.

In the later 1940s Stalin passed "anti-cosmopolitan" laws, which outlawed any interest in the art and heritage of other cultures. He also tried to suppress religious belief, and travel outside the Soviet Union was forbidden. Other Stalinist "reforms" and the ruthless elimination of any opposition created a brutal Soviet regime riddled with bureaucracy and political corruption. Stalin was succeeded by equally hardline Communists to whom the well-being of the Soviet people was less important than Communist ideology.

For Tatjana and others like her, Russia's part in the Allied victory promised much and delivered nothing. It was to be another forty years before *glasnost* (political openness) and *perestroika* (economic change) would tear apart the old ways of the Soviet Union. Critics who had previously been suppressed could now be heard, and this greater openness has at last given the chance of freedom and prosperity to people who have known little of either.